GLORY DAYS

P&O

ORIANA

David L Williams

Ian Allan
PUBLISHING

CONTENTS

First published 1998

ISBN 0 7110 2608 4

Published by Ian Allan Publishing
an imprint of Ian Allan Publishing Ltd, Terminal House, Station Approach, Shepperton, Surrey TW17 8AS.
Printed by Ian Allan Printing Ltd, Riverdene Business Park, Molesey Road, Hersham, Surrey KT12 4RG.

Code: 9811/C

Acknowledgements

I would like to record my appreciation for the assistance received from the following persons and organisations without which this book could not have been realised: Associated Press (Joan Fisher), Michael Cassar, Alex Duncan, Imperial War Museum, Richard de Kerbrech, Lloyd's Shipping Information Services (Norman Hooke), Maritime Photo Library (Adrian Vicary), P&O Steam Navigation Company (Stephen Rabson), the late Tom Rayner, *Southern Daily Echo,* Table Bay Underway Shipping and World Ship Photo Library. I am particularly grateful to Philip Rentell and Ian Shiffmann whose help, respectively, with original printed postcards and with photographs, really made the colour sections of this book possible.

Bibliography

Bathe, Basil, *Seven Centuries of Sea Travel*, Barrie & Jenkins
Braynard, Frank O., *Lives of the Liners*, Cornell Maritime Press
Cable, Boyd, *A Hundred Year History of the P&O*, Ivor Nicholson & Watson
de Kerbrech, Richard P. and Williams, David L., *Damned by Destiny*, Teredo Books
Haws, Duncan, *Merchant Fleets in Profile, Vol 1*, Patrick Stephens
Kludas, Arnold, *Great Passenger Ships of the World, Vols 1-5*, Patrick Stephens
Newell, Gordon, *Ocean Liners of the 20th Century*, Superior Publishing
Rentell, Philip, *Historic P&O-Orient Liners*, Kingfisher Publications
Wall, Robert, *Ocean Liners*, Collins
Williams, David L., *Liners in Battle Dress*, Conway Maritime Press; *Wartime Disasters at Sea*, Patrick Stephens
Wilson, R. M., *The Big Ships*, Cassell

INTRODUCTION

The ocean passenger ship is, without any question of doubt, the greatest of all man-made constructions, especially as exhibited at its peak of development, from the 1930s onwards. They were as large then as any skyscraper or any of the world's greatest railway stations. But unlike those edifices, locked to the earth, static upon their foundations, ocean passenger ships, fitted with machinery as large as that of a power station, were powerful, mobile monuments of man's engineering prowess. Cleaving the waves at anything up to 30kt, they were truly floating cities.

Of course, other, equally large, ocean vessels have been built – large crude oil tankers and aircraft carriers to name just two. Yet none of these has incorporated the same level of complexity or ornamentation as that which is characteristic of the ocean liner. Passengers, as their 'cargo', required creature comforts, as far as possible 'a real home from home' which could delude them into feeling far removed from the ocean's fury (only a hull's thickness away), as if they were still on dry land.

Thus, there was great competition to provide the most luxurious and most extravagant fittings aboard ship possible. The result was magnificent, lavishly decorated cabins and public rooms of a standard that more than favourably compared with the grandest of hotels or stateliest of mansions.

Great Britain was right at the forefront of the introduction and development of the ocean passenger ship and remained the leading force in scheduled passenger ship operation throughout its long era from the early 1840s to the beginning of the 1970s. Over those 130-odd years various companies came and went as they experienced mixed fortunes in this trade which, more than any other, demanded brave investors, innovative engineers and a truly entrepreneurial spirit in order to succeed.

Some famous names arose to dominate the passenger trade and none more so than two British companies, which today are still household names yet which hold the

distinction of having been there at the outset. They were among the earliest pioneers of steam propulsion at sea and are still trading in the ocean passenger business today, albeit now only operating cruises. They are namely the Cunard Steamship Company, founded by Samuel Cunard and partners in 1840 and the Peninsular & Oriental Steam Navigation Company, established in 1837 by Brodie McGhie Willcox and Arthur Anderson. In truth, neither Cunard nor P&O were known originally by their present names but in both cases they are the same company that was launched all those years ago.

Between them, Cunard and P&O have operated no fewer than 700 or so ships (the former 250 and the latter 450), probably a record in itself. Cunard served and dominated the North Atlantic service to the United States and Canada; P&O maintained a complex schedule of routes to India, the Far East and Australasia and was the first choice for the majority of passengers travelling to that part of the globe. Both companies were market leaders in their respective sectors and both set the standard to beat in terms of quality of service, reliability, comfort and safety. It is likely, too, that they were among the very few shipping companies that ever operated profitably, a matter which has, no doubt, largely accounted for their long survival.

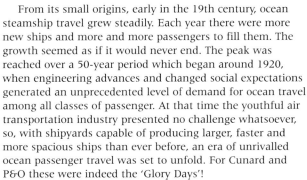

From its small origins, early in the 19th century, ocean steamship travel grew steadily. Each year there were more new ships and more and more passengers to fill them. The growth seemed as if it would never end. The peak was reached over a 50-year period which began around 1920, when engineering advances and changed social expectations generated an unprecedented level of demand for ocean travel among all classes of passenger. At that time the youthful air transportation industry presented no challenge whatsoever, so, with shipyards capable of producing larger, faster and more spacious ships than ever before, an era of unrivalled ocean passenger travel was set to unfold. For Cunard and P&O these were indeed the 'Glory Days'!

Cunard and P&O were, of course, well-established companies by 1920 but they had not yet achieved the status of glory which was ultimately to become associated with them. In this regard the next 50 years were to be significant. 'Glory' certainly implies, if it does not actually mean, such things as excellence, splendour, superiority and renown, all of them accolades which by 1970 were richly deserved by Cunard and P&O, having carried all before them on the ocean highways.

In 1920 P&O was working hard to restore operational normality after the long interruption of hostilities with Germany. Over the course of World War 1, those P&O passenger ships converted for the duration had valiantly flown the national flag as they went about the needs of the country with a commitment to auxiliary duty that paralleled the company's high standards of service in the passenger trade. It was not without its price. War service had cost P&O 13 of its passenger-carrying ships – the sisters *India* and *Persia* in 1915, the *Maloja*, *Simla* and *Arabia* in 1916, the *Ballarat*, *Medina*, *Mongolia*, *Salsette*, *Mooltan* and *Namur* in 1917, and the *Moldavia* and *Marmora* in 1918.

Following the Armistice, P&O embarked upon an aggressive rebuilding programme, supervised personally by Lord Inchcape, the company Chairman, whose inspired guidance and go-ahead policies were highly influential in the company's restoration and growth. By 1930 this had resulted in 20 new additions to the fleet, nothing short of a major expansion. Among them was a new express pair for the

Australia run, the *Maloja* and *Mooltan*, commemorating two of the wartime casualties.

P&O had no intention of standing on its prewar laurels and sought not only to restore its status as the premier line on the routes to the southern Dominions and the Far East but also to build upon its reputation for quality of service, regularity and reliability. Growth of the P&O Group was being achieved not only organically but also by acquisition. On the passenger front, the British India Line, the Union Steamship Company of New Zealand and the New Zealand Shipping Company had all been taken over during the war although each was to retain its separate identity and would continue to be run by its own board of directors. An important additional acquisition made in 1919, which amounted to less than a buy-out but which had enormous long-term strategic value, was the purchase of a large number of Orient Line shares. In fact, P&O was, from that time, the single largest stockholder in Orient. All in all, with these acquisitions, the P&O Group was already by then the dominant force in passenger transport on the routes to the east and to the southern hemisphere in general.

Over the decades to come the emphasis of expansion was to be switched to the P&O fleet itself. Larger and more luxuriously appointed ships were to be progressively introduced offering an unparalleled breadth of service and frequency of sailings. Within 50 years the name P&O was to become, in the public mind, synonymous with ocean travel.

This book, one of a pair (readers may also be interested in the companion title *Glory Days: Cunard*), deals with a timeless, even – as far as the shipping buff is concerned – familiar story. Much has been written on the subject of P&O previously so it contains few surprises, but that is not its purpose. Rather, it is intended to be a celebration in words and pictures of one of Great Britain's greatest passenger shipping companies in the period in which it was at the peak of its ascendancy.

David L. Williams
Newport, Isle of Wight
June 1998

1. SERVICES TO AUSTRALIA, INDIA AND THE FAR EAST – THE 1920s

By 1920, the P&O passenger services were beginning gradually to settle down again after the wartime disruption. Orders for replacement ships had been placed and the vessels returning from war service were being renovated in preparation for the resumption of line voyages. Some ships were, by force of circumstances, given no more than a temporary face-lift while others required a full overhaul and refurbishment immediately.

All this work placed enormous demands on the hard-pressed shipbuilding industry which was struggling to satisfy the requirements of P&O and all the other operators who were seeking to make good the deficiencies in their fleets. In these circumstances, market forces contrived to force up shipyard prices as demand outstripped supply. So exorbitant did shipbuilding costs become that, in 1923, P&O was compelled to postpone part of its rebuilding programme for two years while the situation returned to something closer to normal.

Against this backdrop, P&O was endeavouring to fully reinstate its services via the Suez Canal to India, Australia, New Zealand and the Far East. This involved significant reorganisation of the available ships and, as required, the fleet was supplemented by chartered vessels, some of them former German ships recruited from the reparations organisation. A total of 35 ships from the prewar P&O fleet which had survived the war were returned to service, although 10 were either more than 20 years old or close to reaching that age. Nevertheless, for the next 10 years they filled the gap in P&O's ranks, providing valuable breathing space while new tonnage was being completed. P&O operated a very complex network of routes, not all of which could be described as premier or front-line services. The older ships performed excellently, maintaining these routes until they could be relieved by the replacement vessels as they were introduced. Of course, outside the scope of this type of scheduled service work, P&O also operated a special emigrant service to Australia which will be dealt with separately.

The oldest of the remaining prewar liners was the *Caledonia* built in 1894 which, pre-empting the colour scheme which would be more widely adopted from the 1930s onwards, had entered service with a white-painted hull and buff funnels. The *China* and *Egypt* were the sole survivors of a class which, originally, had comprised five ships, the

A P&O advertisement from November 1928 advertising fortnightly sailings to Australia via the Mediterranean, a scheduled service almost like a cruise itinerary.
P&O Line

▶ The oldest passenger ship in the P&O fleet in 1920 was the *Caledonia*, the vessel which first introduced white livery, in 1894.
Alex Duncan

largest P&O ships at the time of their construction. On 20 May 1922 they were reduced to just one after the *Egypt* was sunk in collision with the French steamship *Seine*, causing 87 deaths and taking more than £1 million of gold bullion with her to the seabed. This was later salvaged in an epic diving feat. The accident occurred off Ushant in thick fog, the *Egypt*, outward bound for Bombay via Marseilles, being struck while she was hove to.

Five of the remaining 'S' class ships – the *Sicilia, Syria, Somali, Soudan* and *Sardinia* – were used to cover the Indian and Far East routes, as were the six surviving vessels of the similar-sized, but later, 'N' class, the *Nyanza, Nore, Nankin, Novara, Nagoya* and *Nellore*. These 11 ships were progressively disposed of between 1923 and 1932, all but the *Nankin* and *Nellore*, which were sold to the Eastern & Australian Steamship Company, going to the scrapyard.

Between 1903 and 1911, P&O had introduced 10 larger ships of the 'M' class, built by Caird & Co, Greenock, Harland & Wolff, Belfast and Barclay Curle, Glasgow. Only four of these elegant, two-funnelled ships had come through the war unscathed. Perhaps the best known of the group, the *Medina*, which had served as Royal Yacht in 1911, taking King George V and Queen Mary to India, had been torpedoed in April 1917, sinking off Start Point. The *Macedonia, Morea, Malwa* and *Mantua* were used on either the

Far Eastern route or the Australian services via Bombay, continuing until the early 1930s when they made way for new ships and were sold for breaking up. The last to go, in May 1935, was the *Mantua*.

Two other classes of passenger ships had been commissioned by P&O in the years prior to World War 1. These were the four 'D' ships, of which three were still available to them in 1920, and the six ships of the very similar 'K' class, none of which had been lost to the enemy. The *Delta, Dongola*, and *Devanha* were returned to the Intermediate service to India, China and Japan for which they had been originally built, sailing from either London or Southampton. Along with Canadian Pacific's *Empress of Australia*, the *Dongola* rendered assistance to the stricken population of Yokohama when a massive earthquake struck the port city on 1 September 1923.

The 'K' class ships *Khiva, Khyber* and *Kashgar* maintained the London to Bombay service from late 1919 to 1923, also making the occasional voyage to Australia. Their consorts, the *Karmala, Kashmir* and *Kalyan* were placed on the Southampton to Australia run but they too interchanged with the Far East service as operational needs dictated. The *Kashmir* had been involved in an unfortunate incident during the later stages of World War 1 while engaged in convoy trooping duties. On 6 October 1918 she had collided with the

Orient Line's *Otranto*, also carrying troops, while they were passing the island of Islay in the most appalling weather. The Orient ship was wrecked with the loss of 431 lives. The six 'K' class ships were disposed of between May 1931 and April 1932, all sold to Japanese shipbreaking firms.

Just one other ship from the pre-World War 1 P&O fleet returned to passenger-carrying duties in 1919 but in her case only briefly for her owners' account. This was the *Kaiser-I-Hind* which had made her maiden voyage from London to Bombay in record time, just under 18 days, commencing on 1 October 1914. She continued with her commercial sailings until 1917 when she was taken over for troopship duties, surviving a U-boat attack thanks to her speed. Returned to P&O at the end of the war, she was chartered to Cunard Line from 8 June 1921 after just two years back on the India run, sailing for it from Southampton to New York. Cunard temporarily renamed her *Emperor of India*, retaining her for about a year. Thereafter with her original name restored,

One of the remaining 'M' class ships, the *Macedonia*. *Maritime Photo Library*

The *Kaiser-I-Hind* in the River Thames, April 1938. *Maritime Photo Library*

The *Narkunda*, 1920, working the India, China and Australian services.
Philip Rentell Collection

The liner *Egypt*, victim of a collision on 20 May 1922.
Ian Allan Library

P. & O. INDIA-CHINA-AUSTRALIA MAIL AND PASSENGER SERVICES.

S.S. "NARKUNDA" { 16,000 TONS. 20,000 H.P.

P&O placed her once more on the route to India via the Suez Canal, a service she continued to fulfil for another 16 years.

None of the 28 passenger ships so far briefly described was especially distinctive or celebrated in its own right but they characterised the type which had gained for P&O its reputation as a passenger carrier: steady, dependable and comfortable. Their accommodation, while not lavish, was pleasant and attractive, laid out to take account of the tropical climates in which they operated for much of the time. Importantly for P&O, their contribution in the difficult period of the 1920s was to form the foundation on which future progress was to be built.

Lord Inchcape, the P&O Chairman, took a direct and personal interest in the fleet rebuilding programme of the 1920s, making the decisions as to when orders could proceed so as to take most advantage of more favourable shipyard prices. His involvement extended to such matters as developing the policy for the company's front-line ships and the selection of innovative propulsion systems and other features when this was deemed appropriate.

The *Naldera* and *Narkunda*, the first new passenger ships to join the P&O fleet after World War 1, were in fact designed before the war and ordered in 1913. The outbreak of war delayed their entry into service, but they were launched respectively on 29 December 1917 and 25 April 1918 with the intention of rapid completion for employment as either Armed Merchant Cruisers, troopships or even

aircraft carriers. None of this transpired, however, for they were not completed until March 1920 and then in the form originally intended. Not only were the *Naldera* and *Narkunda* the first three-funnelled ships owned by P&O, they were also, at more than 16,000 gross tons each, the largest. The *Naldera* also happened to be the last vessel of a long line of ships built for P&O by Caird & Co of Greenock.

They entered the express mail service to India or Australia via the Suez Canal, the *Naldera* making her first sailing from Tilbury to Sydney on 24 March 1920 with the *Narkunda* following her just six days later, making her first voyage to Bombay. They marked the first big step forward in the enhancement of passenger facilities on the run to the southern Dominions. Their public spaces were a marked improvement on anything previously available, being both stylish and smart.

The *Narkunda* made her first sailing from London to Sydney on 9 July 1920. Thereafter, the sister ships alternated between the Indian and Australian services until 1931 when they were permanently transferred to the London, Bombay and Far East route following the entry into service of the first of the 'Strath' class of ships.

The commissioning of the next pair in 1923, the two-funnelled *Mooltan* and *Maloja* for the Australian express service, was an important milestone in the growth of the P&O fleet, for they were the first vessels owned by the company which exceeded 20,000 gross tons. The dimensions

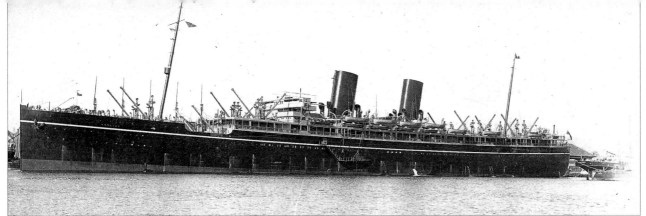

The first 20,000-ton liners for the Bombay and Australia mail service, the *Mooltan*...
Ian Allan Library

...and the *Maloja*, a photograph taken in September 1937.
Maritime Photo Library

voyaging through tropical waters from that time. They were noted for the quality of their second-class spaces when companies more typically concentrated their attention on the higher grades of accommodation. They were also renowned for their seaworthiness and steadiness in all weathers.

Unusually for first-rate ships, at a time when the geared steam turbine was gaining popularity as the preferred propulsion system for express passenger liners, the *Mooltan* and *Maloja* retained steam reciprocating machinery, probably because of its inherent reliability and economy on long runs.

The *Maloja* made her maiden voyage to Bombay and back in November 1923, transferring to the Australia route from 18 January 1924. From 1929, Bombay became a regular port of call for all P&O ships on the run to Australia. The *Mooltan's* maiden voyage took her from London to Colombo, Melbourne and Sydney, departing Tilbury on 21 December 1923.

For all the dependability of their quadruple expansion steam machinery, the *Mooltan* and *Maloja* were relatively slow ships, barely capable of achieving the 17kt speed stipulated for the mail contracts. In 1929 they were taken in hand for engine improvements as part of an enhancement programme which involved many of the other, new, P&O ships. The *Mooltan* was fitted with an auxiliary low-pressure turbo-electric plant while the *Maloja* had a supplementary low-pressure turbine installed. In both cases, service speed was increased to 17.5kt.

of the Suez Canal had in a sense acted as the regulator of the maximum size of the passenger vessels heading east which worked this route. The requirements of wartime operations had promoted developments to the canal permitting larger vessels to make the passage but the *Mooltan* and *Maloja* were still the largest ships possible that were capable of navigating the Suez Canal.

The pair featured the open promenade decks extending around the stern which became characteristic of P&O vessels

More P&O postcard
impressions from the
1920s: the *Mooltan*...
Philip Rentell Collection

...the *Cathay*, a card
published by the County
Hotel, Newcastle-on-Tyne...
Philip Rentell Collection

P. & O. S.S. CATHAY, 15,000 TONS GROSS.
Australia Mail and Passenger Service.

P. & O. INDIA-CHINA-AUSTRALIA MAIL AND PASSENGER SERVICES.

S.S. "MONGOLIA" | 16,000 TONS. | 13,000 H.P.

P. & O. S.S. RANPURA, 16,600 TONS GROSS.
India Mail and Passenger Service.

...the turbine steamer *Mongolia,* her counter stern appearing old fashioned at a time when the trend was towards cruiser sterns...
Philip Rentell Collection

...and the *Ranpura.*
Philip Rentell Collection

In 1923 P&O introduced its first geared steam turbine ships, the very similar *Moldavia* and *Mongolia* but it was a short-lived experiment. Carrying some 220 first-class and 175 second-class passengers each, the *Moldavia* and *Mongolia* were placed on the Intermediate Australian service from Tilbury, calling at Marseilles, Port Said, Colombo, Fremantle, Adelaide, Melbourne and Sydney. From 1928, after a refit, the second-class accommodation was downgraded to tourist or third-class. At the same time, the *Moldavia* alone was fitted with a second, dummy funnel which did little for her appearance but helped to distinguish her from her close partner. In 1931, both the *Moldavia* and *Mongolia* became tourist-only ships with accommodation for a total of 840 passengers in a single class.

The P&O fleet rebuilding programme gathered pace from 1925. Between then and 1930, no fewer than nine premier passenger ships were commissioned. There was a class of four 16,000-tonners for the Indian and Far East routes and three new vessels for the Australian intermediate service, the *Cathay*, *Comorin* and *Chitral*.

First out was the *Razmak*, a one-off ship, for employment on the Aden to Bombay shuttle, built as a replacement for the *Salsette*, which had been torpedoed and sunk on 20 July 1917. The last P&O passenger vessel to have a counter stern, her first sailing to take her on station at Aden commenced from London on 13 March 1925. In 1926 the shuttle route to Bombay was extended from Marseilles but, after only two or so more years, P&O discontinued the service altogether when

the Australia and Far East routes were combined between Suez and Bombay. Later, in 1930, the *Razmak* was sold to the Union Steamship Company of New Zealand for trans-Pacific duties as the *Monowai*. She replaced her new owner's *Tahiti* which had been lost on 17 August 1930 after foundering in the mid-Pacific. Catastrophic engine failure had ruptured her hull and watertight bulkheads causing fatal leaks.

Reverting to quadruple expansion steam engines, P&O next introduced the *Ranpura*, *Ranchi*, *Rawalpindi* and *Rajputana* between April 1925 and January 1926. The first two were placed on the Bombay direct service from Tilbury, the latter pair entering the Far East service to China and Japan. Although outwardly they looked identical, there were, of course, minor differences among the quartet.

Hard on their heels came the slightly smaller but outwardly not dissimilar *Cathay*, *Comorin* and *Chitral*, upgrading the Australian Intermediate service. They were to be interchangeable between the Australian and Far East routes, filling in between the express vessels. Upon the arrival of the '*Straths*' they too were transferred permanently to the Far East run. Their introduction permitted the resumption of fortnightly sailings to Australia from 1925. Prior to then it had been a monthly schedule.

The passenger accommodation in all classes on these ships was located on or above the upper deck. Like the '*R*' class before them, the three '*C*'s were completed with steam reciprocating main machinery. With the exception of the

Cathay, all the ships of both groups received engine modifications in the period 1930 to 1931, having an additional low-pressure turbine installed in order to improve their speed.

Neither the *Ranpura* and her sisters or the three 'C' class ships offered the ostentatiously appointed public spaces that were typical of many of the liners operating the North Atlantic service but they did provide a standard of accommodation which was both comfortable and pleasantly attractive. It was also significantly superior to that which had been available on these routes before World War 1 and, even, aboard the older ships of the early 1920s, all part of P&O's continuing effort to deliver higher standards on all the services of its route network.

For all of these new P&O vessels, the passenger numbers were relatively low for ships of their size and this was even more true of the larger *Mooltan* and *Maloja*. Apart from the carriage of passengers, these liners also earned considerable revenue transporting cargo on whichever routes they operated. Reflecting this, they were all provided with substantial cargo capacity.

With their distinctive colouring, twin black funnels, buff upperworks and black hulls lined in white, there was a certain family likeness between the *Mooltan* and *Maloja*, the four 'R' class ships and the three 'C' vessels and they were instantly recognisable wherever they were seen.

The building programme of the 1920s culminated in P&O's crowning achievement of the decade, the stately and traditionally styled *Viceroy of India* whose engines were a radical departure from contemporary practice. Originally ordered under the name *Taj Mahal*, an equally fitting identity, she went a long way to elevating the quality of service on the India route to the standard by now established for the Antipodean trade. P&O was not given to making revolutionary changes, generally leaving innovation to others while it pursued tried and proven practices. But in the case of the *Viceroy of India*, P&O took the bold and unprecedented step of adopting turbo-electric machinery, making her only the third passenger vessel in the world to have such an installation – she was just beaten into service by two similarly-engined units of a Panama Pacific trio, the *California* and *Virginia*. Launched on 15 September 1928 at Alexander Stephen's Glasgow shipyard, the *Viceroy of India* made her maiden voyage on the Bombay direct service on 7 March 1929. The third American vessel, the *Pennsylvania*, followed her just four months later.

Compared with the other passenger ships in the P&O fleet, the *Viceroy of India* was a fast ship, having a service

▼ The shuttle service liner *Razmak* replaced the *Salsette* which had been torpedoed in World War 1.
Ian Allan Library

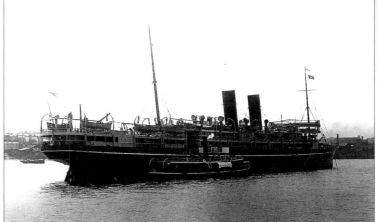

The revolutionary *Viceroy of India*. Aboard her, for the first time, all first class passengers had cabins to themselves.
Philip Rentell Collection

▶

& O. S.S. VICEROY OF INDIA, 19,700 TONS GROSS.
India Mail and Passenger Service.

The four new ships introduced to the India and the Far East services were the *Ranchi*...
Ian Allan Library

▼

...the *Ranpura*, a 1935 picture...
Maritime Photo Library

...the *Rajputana*...
Ian Allan Library

...and the *Rawalpindi*.
Alex Duncan

speed of 19kt. In September 1932 she broke the record for the run to India, making the passage in 16 days, 1hr and 42min.

The accommodation aboard the *Viceroy of India* was truly astounding for a ship of her size, the staterooms in first-class being especially noteworthy. But the quality of her appointments was not restricted to the higher grade passengers alone. P&O had endeavoured and, for that matter, succeeded, in designing the interiors of what, for them, was a ground-breaking vessel, such that comparable advances were made in the level of comfort enjoyed by all classes in the cabins and facilities throughout the ship.

The restoration of the P&O passenger services had been the challenge of the 1920s – an accomplishment fulfilled. The decade to follow was to see these achievements taken to greater heights as even more, exciting new vessels were added to the fleet strength.

A bold experiment of the late 1920s: the turbo-electric *Viceroy of India* in trials views taken for promotional purposes by British Thompson Houston. *Ian Allan Library*

942

2. THE BRANCH LINE SERVICE

P&O had long been interested in breaking into the Australian emigrant service via Cape Town, indeed it had been a prime objective of the company as far back as the 19th century. In January 1910, P&O purchased the goodwill and fleet of five remaining passenger ships of Wilhelm Lund's Blue Anchor Line which was still reeling from the loss, the previous July, in mysterious circumstances, of its new flagship *Waratah*.

The new group was named the P&O Branch Service to Australia or more simply the Branch Line, inaugurated on 15 September 1910 by the *Commonwealth*. The Blue Anchor Line itself disappeared completely as a company soon after P&O's acquisition, being wound up after going into voluntary liquidation. The Branch Service was operated as a separate entity, distinct from the rest of the P&O fleet and, until March 1914, the ships continued to wear the Blue Anchor funnel colours and fly the Lund houseflag at the foremast. However, the white hull band, characteristic of P&O's style of livery, was added to their black hulls. From 1914, the emigrant ships, including five new, specially designed vessels, ordered in November 1910, adopted P&O's plain black funnels and from that time all remaining traces of Blue Anchor disappeared.

After World War 1, only the *Commonwealth* remained with P&O as the only survivor of the original ships acquired from Blue Anchor. Besides her, the *Borda, Beltana, Benalla* and *Berrima* of the new ships ordered in 1910 had survived the war. With the resurgence of the emigrant trade, these five ships were pressed back into service at the earliest opportunity, resuming the Australian run via Cape Town with the exception of the *Beltana* which now sailed via the Suez Canal. The four 'B' class ships, single-funnel, counter-sterned vessels with quadruple expansion, steam reciprocating engines, had been evolved specially to provide intending settlers with comfortable and affordable travel. They provided accommodation for up to 1,100 third-class passengers in a single grade of accommodation. Of these,

permanent berths were provided for only 350, the cabin space for the remaining 750 being organised on a seasonal basis as passenger manifests dictated.

Each of these ships had been allocated the names of Australian places, in each case beginning with a 'B' to indicate that the vessels worked the Branch Line service.

The *Commonwealth* was disposed of for scrap in 1923, by then 21 years old and incompatible with the other ships on the route. The four old 'B' class ships continued to maintain the service through the 1920s and into the 1930s, being eventually replaced as a new class of 'B' steamers, ordered from 1920 and all built by Harland & Wolff, progressively came onstream.

The lead ship, *Baradine*, made her maiden voyage to Australia on 21 September 1921, followed on 27 January 1922 by the *Ballarat* which was named in honour of the single original 'B' class ship lost in World War 1. The third new 'B' ship, the *Balranald* left London on her maiden Australian trip on 5 April 1922. Next came the *Bendigo* on 9 August of the same year with the *Barrabool* bringing up the rear, her delivery on 30 March 1923 completing the group.

The new vessels were some 2,000 gross tons bigger than their predecessors but they had similar passenger numbers, suggesting marginally improved, rather more spacious, accommodation for the emigrant traveller. Like the earlier 'B' class, the berths were a mixture of permanent and temporary, providing for approximately 490 of the former and around 740 of the latter. They retained quadruple expansion machinery, permitting a comfortable service speed of 13-14kt but in 1929 engine modifications were carried out in keeping with the process of upgrade to other vessels of P&O's main passenger fleet. The addition of a Bauer-Wach exhaust turbine increased their speed by just over a knot.

From this time, the Branch Line service was split, with the *Ballarat* along with the older *Beltana* making regular sailings via Suez, including a call at Malta. The other new ships remained on the Cape route until after the completion

of their engine upgrades when all five worked the run to Australia via the Suez Canal leaving the older vessels to make the longer passage around the Cape. The arrival of the new 'B' class ships and the changing needs of the emigrant trade permitted P&O to gradually dispose of the older vessels when there was no longer capacity to support nine ships. First to go were the *Borda* and *Beltana* in April and May 1930 respectively. The *Beltana* was sold for proposed conversion into a whale factory ship but this never transpired. The *Borda* was broken up in Japan as were the *Berrima* from September 1930 and the *Benalla* from January 1931.

As things turned out, the later class did not survive very much longer either. The formation of the Aberdeen & Commonwealth Line in 1928, which was operating refurbished one-class ships via the Suez Canal, had already forced P&O to switch its vessels to this route from 1929, first alternately and then completely. The fact was that Aberdeen & Commonwealth's green-hulled 'Bay'-class ships now offered a better standard of accommodation than the P&O 'B' class. Unable to compete with these upgraded ships without investing in similar refurbishments to its own vessels and with the decline in the emigrant trade not supporting this kind of costly outlay, P&O elected instead to suspend the Branch Line service altogether from 1936.

◄ P&O's Branch Line service promoted in a poster from the late 1920s after the route had been split. The fares were very low by the standards of that time but were still higher than the post-World War 2 assisted passage rate. *P&O Line*

◄ A rather faded postcard depicting one of the ships of the pre-World War 1 'B' class, from a painting by William L. Wyllie. *Philip Rentell Collection*

◄◄ Two ships of the first 'B' class, the *Beltana*... *World Ship Photo Library*

◄ ...and the *Berrima*, seen at Cape Town. *Alex Duncan*

Simultaneously, the *Moldavia* and *Mongolia* were modified to provide more low-cost accommodation. After World War 2, a number of vessels would be requisitioned and adapted specially for the carriage of settlers to Australasia. Later, as the large, express ships approached the ends of their careers, they would successively be converted into single-class tourist ships, making provision for the continuing Australian emigrant trade.

The parade to the block came swiftly and within five to six years the 'B' class ships and the Branch Service were no more. Unlike the earlier 'Bs' they were broken up in the United Kingdom, probably a more politically preferable destination given the warlike noises emanating from the Far East. The *Ballarat* was dismantled at Briton Ferry, South Wales commencing 27 May 1935, the *Bendigo* at Barrow-in-Furness from 6 May 1936. The *Balranald*, at Troon, and the *Baradine* at Dalmuir were next to be sold off for breaking up, in June 1936. It was left to the *Barrabool* to make the last departure from London to Sydney, closing the chapter on the P&O Branch Service for emigrants heading 'Down Under'. Her fate was sealed on 31 July when she arrived at Bo'ness on the Firth of Forth where she too was broken up for scrap.

In their day, the Branch Line and the unique 'B' class steamers specially designed for the service had substantially elevated the quality of emigrant passages to the southern Dominions, reflecting the value P&O attached to this important trade.

The vessels of the second 'B' class could be distinguished by their shorter forecastle and the twin ventilators extending up above the bridge front. This is the *Balranald*. *World Ship Photo Library*

The *Barrabool* of 1923 berthed at Cape Town. *World Ship Photo Library*

The *Ballarat*, leadship of the second 'B' class.
Alex Duncan

The *Baradine* making her departure from Table Bay.
Alex Duncan

Indicating the route switch of the Branch Service, this card of the *Bendigo* has been overprinted with Egypt and Ceylon, even though the vessel is shown against the backdrop of the Table Mountain.
Philip Rentell Collection

A Frank H. Mason picture of the *Ballarat* of the second, larger 'B' class.
Philip Rentell Collection

3. SERVICES TO AUSTRALIA, INDIA AND THE FAR EAST – THE 1930s

The crowning glory of P&O's continuing fleet expansion in the 1930s, building on the foundation laid down in the previous decade, was the commissioning of the five 'Strath' liners, collectively known as the 'White Sisters'.

They introduced yet higher standards to the Australian mail service and are remembered with affection by former passengers and crew members alike. Though considered as a class of sister-ships, the quintet were not identical, in effect constituting three different types, each incorporating improvements derived from experience operating the earlier ships.

Vickers Armstrong at Barrow in Furness, Cumbria was responsible for all five ships. The lead pair, the *Strathnaver* and *Strathaird*, were ordered early in the 1930s as both the culminating achievement and swansong of the Lord Inchcape era of regeneration. The first of the duo, the *Strathnaver*, entered service on the Australia mail run on 2 October 1931, affording the elderly company Chairman the opportunity of seeing the product of his prescient and ambitious policies for the company's future prior to his death in 1932. She had been launched the previous February. In Lord Inchcape's successor, his son-in-law, Lord Craigmyle, the Hon Alexander Shaw, a new champion for the bold plan for P&O's continued growth was to take over at the top. Equally forward-looking and positive, he sought for the company a position of acclaim on the Eastern and Australian routes such as that associated with Cunard on the North Atlantic.

The *Strathaird*, second of the new pair, commenced her maiden voyage to Australia from London, via Bombay and Colombo on 12 February 1932. The *Strathnaver* and *Strathaird* were imposing ships with all-white hulls and buff funnels, reintroducing the colour scheme briefly tried many years earlier with the *Caledonia* in 1894 and the prewar *Salsette* of the Aden shuttle service. Each had three funnels, the only class of P&O ships, apart from the *Naldera* and *Narkunda*, to have this many, although two of the funnels, the

P. & O. Electric Ship STRATHNAVER, 22,500 TONS.
Carrying First-class and Tourist-class Passengers.
India and Australia Mail Service.

forwardmost and aftmost, were dummies which would be removed later in their careers.

Benefiting from the positive operational experience gained with the *Viceroy of India* and reinforcing P&O's willingness to be radical whenever appropriate, turbo-electric drive was also selected as the main propulsion machinery. This was considered the most ideal arrangement given the intention to employ them on cruises as well as on regular services. Service speed on the London to Sydney run was 21kt. The public spaces aboard the *Strathnaver* and *Strathaird* reflected the steadily improving standards introduced in all of the front-line ships built since World War 1 but which had been enhanced so dramatically in the interiors of the *Viceroy of India*. For those making the passage to Australia, the

▲ It is not difficult to imagine how striking in appearance the *Strathnaver* must have seemed when she first entered service.
Philip Rentell Collection

spaciousness, comfort and overall standards of decoration were unsurpassed.

Prior to the inauguration of the first and second vessels of the 'Strath' class, two additional, smaller ships for the Far East routes were delivered to replace the final 'K' class steamers, both having been laid down at the Alexander Stephen shipyard in Glasgow in 1930. Named *Carthage* and *Corfu*, they were graceful twin-funnelled vessels of approximately 14,000 gross tons fitted with steam turbine engines and capable of 18kt service speed. The *Corfu* was launched on 20 May 1931, commencing her first line voyage on 16 October of the same year. The *Carthage* followed in the same season, launched on 18 August and making her maiden voyage from London that 28 November.

Accommodation aboard the *Carthage* and *Corfu* provided for approximately 375 passengers in two classes. As testified in a postcard sent on the maiden voyage of the *Corfu*, these ships were 'a great improvement on the old type of P&O boats'. Interestingly, although they were relatively small vessels, they were among the first passenger ships to have permanent open air swimming pools, a welcome facility, no doubt offering a cooling relief on the long passage across the Indian Ocean and through the South China Sea, most of it routed along or close to the Equator.

In the *Carthage* and *Corfu*, the traditional P&O livery of black hull and funnels with stone-coloured upperworks was retained.

As hinted, the further upgrade to the P&O fleet arising from the commissioning of the *Strathnaver*, *Strathaird*, *Carthage* and *Corfu* provided the opportunity to dispose of more of the older tonnage. Three vessels of the 'K' class reciprocating steam ships, the *Karmala*, *Kashmir* and *Kashgar*, along with remaining units of the preceding 'M' and 'N' groups of ships, were sold for breaking up in this period.

The third of the 'Strath' ships, essentially a one-off, was launched at Barrow on 4 April 1935 by the Duchess of York, later Queen Elizabeth the Queen Mother. This was the elegant *Strathmore* which incorporated a number of modifications compared with the earlier pair. The result established a characteristic P&O appearance that it could be argued was reflected in all of the future, large passenger vessels of the fleet that entered service up to the *Arcadia* and *Iberia* of 1954.

For the *Strathmore*, P&O decided to revert to geared steam

First of the 'White Sisters', the *Strathnaver* on builder's trials in 1931.
Ian Allan Library

The *Strathnaver* in drydock showing off the open promenade decks extending around her stern.
Ian Allan Library

turbine propulsion, indeed the short-lived experiment with turbo-electric machinery ended with the *Strathnaver* and *Strathaird*, at least in that era. The reason for this change is not known but it may have been dictated by a need for a measure of standardisation as engine-room staff transferring between ships required experience of a wide range of propulsion systems. That said, in the late 1930s, the P&O fleet featured vessels with steam reciprocating, steam-turbine and turbo-electric drive systems as well as diesel power which was being adopted increasingly for the new cargo ships then entering service. Besides this, no attempt was made to re-engine either of the original 'Straths' or the *Viceroy of India*.

What mattered was that the *Strathmore* was a fast ship. She broke the London to Bombay speed record, averaging over 20kt over the passage and reducing the Marseilles to Bombay leg to just 10 days.

The *Strathmore* had a single, centrally placed, funnel. Its somewhat shorter length compared with the funnels installed on the subsequent *Stratheden* and *Strathallan* was one of the few features that helped to distinguish her from her later half-sisters. She could accommodate a total of 1,025 passengers in a standard of comfort and commodiousness, if not luxury, comparable to that of the *Strathnaver* and *Strathaird*.

Her public rooms were beautifully appointed, modern and light but nevertheless exhibiting a quality of workmanship and style which was of the highest order. She was said to be more luxurious than the similar-sized Orient liner *Orion* which was her contemporary.

The *Strathmore's* first sailing on 4 October 1935 took her on the first of a series of cruises prior to entering the London to Australia express mail service in November, the beginning of the high season on the run 'Down Under'. Just under two years later, the fourth ship in the loosely-defined class, the *Stratheden*, entered the water for the first time on 10 June 1937. Her maiden voyage to Australia via Bombay commenced on 24 December 1937, three months almost to the day after the launch of the fifth and final ship, the *Strathallan*. The *Strathallan's* maiden sailing, on 18 March 1938, completed the programme of upgrade to the front-line

928

express ships, every P&O route from that time having modern tonnage operating on it.

Slightly bigger, at just under 24,000 gross tons, than the *Strathmore,* which was again slightly larger and longer than the inaugural '*Strath*' ships, the *Stratheden* and *Strathallan* were very similar in appearance, distinguished by their taller funnels and greater areas of open promenade deck. Single-reduction geared turbines driving twin screws gave them a service speed of 20kt, the five ships together now able to maintain a regular timetable of departures, with sailings every other week from London and Sydney.

Passenger space on the *Stratheden* and *Strathallan* was lower than on the *Strathmore,* comprising 530 first-class and 450 tourist-class. Once again, the public rooms were elegant but refined, exhibiting a propriety that ensured comfortable, tasteful and relaxing surroundings for passengers which at the same time were neither overpowering nor excessively ostentatious.

The arrival of the *Stratheden* and *Strathallan* triggered off further disposals as P&O's fleet modernisation reached its climax. The *Moldavia* made her final Australian voyage on 17 September 1937. She was then laid up until sold for scrap on 18 April 1938. By contrast, the similar *Mongolia* was chartered to the New Zealand Shipping Company from

P&O poster featuring the 'White Sisters', *Strathaird* and *Strathnaver.*
P&O Line

▲

The *Strathaird,* consort to the *Strathnaver.*
Ian Allan Library

▶

P. & O. R.M.S. STRATHMORE, 23,500 TONS.
*Carrying First-class and Tourist-class Passengers
India and Australia Mail Service.*

BERNARD W. CHURCH

◀ The *Strathmore*.
Philip Rentell Collection

◀ Half-sister *Stratheden*, a
painting by Bernard
W. Church.
Philip Rentell Collection

P&O's three turbo-electric passenger liners together at Tilbury prior to the *Strathaird's* maiden voyage in February 1932. From left to right: *Strathaird*, *Strathnaver* and *Viceroy of India*.
Ian Allan Library

More new ships for the Far East service, the *Carthage* and... *Ian Allan Library* ▶

...the *Corfu*, a card posted on her maiden voyage by a passenger bound for Malaya.
David L. Williams Collection ▶

The turbine-powered *Strathmore*, third of the 'Strath' liners but essentially a one-off ship.
Ian Allan Library

Launch of the *Stratheden* on 10 June 1937.
P&O Line

7 May 1938 who renamed her *Rimutaka*. Whereas the *Mongolia's* fate had brought the curtain down on an all too brief career, the change of destiny for the *Mongolia* spelled the start of an extension to her service life of greater duration than the years she had accumulated up to that time. After several metamorphoses, she was still going strong as the *Acapulco* in the 1960s.

The continued survival of the *Naldera* and *Narkunda*, both postwar new deliveries but whose designs were of prewar vintage, now also came under close scrutiny. But as with the *Moldavia* and *Mongolia*, fate was to treat the two ships differently. While on the one hand the *Naldera* was sent immediately for breaking up at Bo'ness in November 1938, the *Narkunda* was almost simultaneously sent back to the shipyard for conversion from coal-burning to oil-firing. She was destined to give P&O another year of service as a passenger liner before falling victim in the ensuing war while valiantly undertaking auxiliary duties. Making her the last casualty of the P&O passenger fleet in the run up to World War 2, the veteran *Kaiser-I-Hind* was broken up at Blyth, Northumberland from April 1938.

One final new passenger ship was set to join P&O before the clouds of war rolled in, bringing scheduled services to a halt until the late 1940s. This was the twin-screw steamship *Canton,* a larger single-funnelled version of the *Carthage* and *Corfu*. When she first entered service she still wore the traditional black and stone P&O colours, the last new P&O ship to be so painted, only to be given the new white hull and buff funnel livery within a year of her introduction. A further year on she would be repainted yet again, this time navy grey.

The fourth ship to bear the name, the *Canton* was launched on 14 April 1938, making her maiden voyage from Tilbury to Singapore, Hong Kong and Yokohama via Suez on 7 October 1938. At just under 16,000 gross tons, powered by single-reduction geared steam turbines giving her a service speed of 18kt, she could carry 546 passengers in two classes. Like all the P&O passenger ships of this period she was well appointed, her recreational spaces featuring a large games deck and an open-air pool.

In 1920 the P&O passenger fleet had comprised 41 ships

aggregating 360,000 gross tons, the majority more than 25 years old, the newest having been commissioned in that very year. By 1939, just under 20 years later, P&O had commissioned 39 new ships of 461,625 gross tons, 23 of which were passenger vessels. Over the same period, 29 ships of 240,000 gross tons had been disposed of, most of them going for scrap. The passenger fleet numbers had reduced to 19 vessels, all modern, although their aggregate tonnage was little less at 345,000 than the 41 steamships of 20 years earlier. Passenger numbers along with grades of fare and standards of accommodation had also changed noticeably for the better.

It remained to be seen how many of this modern fleet of ships would survive the rigours of the war at sea only to renew their contribution to P&O's growing reputation after the cessation of hostilities. The interwar years had been a glorious period in the expansion of P&O as an ocean passenger carrier. Now its record of achievement was to receive further acclaim for quite different reasons, as P&O vessels upheld the proud traditions of the British Merchant Marine, serving their country just as they had served their owner. And though it was not known at that time, the period that was to follow would see P&O reach its zenith as one of the greatest British passenger shipping companies of all time.

'Travel by P&O – Straits, China, Japan', a P&O poster from July 1932. *P&O Line*

O. R.M.S. CARTHAGE, 15,000 TONS GROSS.
India and Far Eastern Mail Service.

The *Carthage* with, in the background, a British India Line ship, either the *Talamba* or the *Tairea*. *Philip Rentell Collection*

A superb detailed view of
the *Stratheden* lying at
anchor.
Ian Allan Library

Last of the group and least
lucky of the quintet, the
short-lived *Strathalla*n.
P&O Line

The *Canton* as first delivered
with black hull and funnel.
P&O Line

4. CRUISING AND TROOPING

Apart from the scheduled service operations for which it was best known, there were two other important dimensions to the P&O passenger shipping enterprise – luxury off-peak cruising and Government trooping. The latter was a peacetime activity which involved the transportation of units of the Regular Army to and from military outposts of the Empire which, at that time, still extended across the globe.

P&O had been among the earliest shipping companies to offer pleasure cruises, diverting ships to this work during the low season months for regular traffic or by organising excursions based on segments of scheduled passages. Indeed, one of P&O's elegant, early steamships, the three-masted *Ceylon* of 1858, received acclaim as an 'exclusive cruising yacht' although its principal period of employment as a cruise vessel, from 1881, was after the ship had passed on from P&O ownership.

The *Viceroy of India*, another trials photograph of the celebrated liner.
Ian Allan Library

Flashback to 1911, P&O
cruises aboard the *Vectis*, a
hint of things to come.
P&O Line

P&O's main diversion into cruising prior to the 1920s had
been between 1904 and 1912 when the elegant two-
funnelled, twin-screw steamer *Rome*, then 23 years old, was
converted permanently for cruise work and renamed *Vectis*.
She offered between 10 and 12 cruises a year to an exclusive
clientéle of just 150 first-class passengers visiting the Baltic,
North Africa, the Atlantic isles, the Adriatic and the Holy
Land. These were generally organised so that the visits to
northern waters were made during the warmer summer
months and, for the comfort of her passengers, the reverse in

the winter, making the trips to southern climes at that time
of year.

By the 1920s, cruising was not as significant an element
of P&O's passenger ship operations as it was, say, for the
Orient Line. It was not really until the postwar rebuilding
programme had been completed, allowing the full
restoration of all P&O's scheduled services to India, the Far
East and Australia, that any capacity became available to
undertake excursion work to any extent.

The trend was essentially reintroduced with the four
ships of the 'R' class. Each year, during the low season they
offered a number of cruises, mainly to the Mediterranean.
With the *Viceroy of India*, a more planned programme of
cruises was launched as a regular feature of her annual
operations rather than as a casual, infrequent affair – a
convenient expedient determined to be necessary through
poor fortunes in her main 'raison d'être'. The beautifully
appointed *Viceroy of India* could offer the quality and range of
facilities that readily lent themselves to holidays at sea (a
permanent swimming pool for instance) and she was both
popular and a great success as a cruise liner.

In her first season, immediately following her maiden
voyage on the Indian mail route, she made five
Mediterranean tours between May and August 1929.
Thereafter, throughout the 1930s she continued to offer a
selection of appealing cruise itineraries based at
Southampton.

When they entered service from 1931, the white-hulled
Strathnaver and *Strathaird* perpetuated the arrangements
established with the *Viceroy of India* and they, too, became
popular cruising ships when engaged on this work between
their regular sailings on the Australia run.

It was considered that the turbo-electric machinery
installations of the 'Strath' pair and the *Viceroy of India* were
ideally suited for the enormously varied demands of gently
paced cruising on the one hand and high-speed line voyages
on the other. In basic terms, in all three cases, their twin
screws were directly driven by synchronous electrical motors
attached to the propeller shafts, the current being generated
by turbo alternators, each complete installation supplied by
British Thomson-Houston. The advantage of this

P. & O. S.S. VICEROY OF INDIA, 19,700 TONS GROSS.

India Mail and Passenger Service.

MAGIC NIGHTS

MERRY DAYS

P & O

CRUISES

SPRINGTIME
in the
MEDITERRANEAN

The P. & O. attractive booklet giving details of twenty Spring and Summer Cruises may be had on application.

By S.S. Moldavia, 17,000 tons :

APRIL 9   To Athens, Istanbul, Santorin, etc. 23 days, Tourist Class, from £23.

MAY 9   To Barcelona, Palma, Algiers, etc. 14 days Tourist Class, from £14.

By S.S. Strathnaver, 22,500 tons :

MAY 15   To Egypt and Palestine. 21 days, 1st Class from £33 : Tourist Class from £20.

P&O

1A, COCKSPUR ST., LONDON, S.W.1
134, LEADENHALL ST., LONDON, E.C.3
AUSTRALIA HOUSE, STRAND, W.C.2
or Local Agents

◄◄ The *Viceroy of India* was an especially popular P&O cruise liner in the early 1930s.
Philip Rentell Collection

◄ 'Magic Nights, Merry Days', the programme of springtime cruises in the Mediterranean by the *Moldavia* and *Strathnaver*.
P&O Line

arrangement, apart from freeing up engine-room space normally required for reverse gearing, reverse rotation of the screws being simply achieved by the reversal of the electrical current flow, was that it suited the contrasting requirements of economical cruising speeds and the faster performance dictated by adherence to a route timetable.

Cruising afforded a new lease of life, too, for the *Moldavia* and *Mongolia* in the 1930s. When they were not employed on the Intermediate service to Australia they were engaged making pleasure trips and proved to be popular when performing these duties.

At the other end of the passenger shipping spectrum, P&O's participation in Government troop transportation for the Ministry of Transport had steadily declined from the early part of the century when political situations and colonial incidents in East and South Africa, India and the Far East had dictated a heavy work-load for the vessels engaged in this activity.

Back at the turn of the 19th century, P&O had introduced three new purpose-built vessels for Government trooping: the *Assaye*, *Sobraon* and *Plassy*. These ships maintained the service in conjunction with similar trooper types operated by

the Bibby Line and the British India Line. The *Sobraon* was an early casualty, stranded off Foochow in dense fog on 21 April 1901 while bound for Shanghai on only her third voyage. The *Assaye* and *Plassy* went on to give valuable service, reverting to hospital ships during World War 1.

After the war, they resumed their peacetime troop-carrying duties for the Government, the *Plassy* continuing until July 1924 when she was sold for breaking up in Italy. The *Assaye* lasted somewhat longer, being disposed of in May 1928, also for breaking up but in her case in Norway.

For the first time in over half a century, for an interlude of 10 years, P&O had no vessels engaged in troop transportation work, the Government relying on Bibby's prewar 'Shire' class steamers, and British India's *Neuralia* and *Nevasa* for the accomplishment of these duties.

In the run-up to World War 2, the Government determined to commission a new class of permanent troopships to replace all the remaining older vessels of this type and to raise generally the standard of accommodation for troops travelling overseas. The four-ship class was designated for operation by Bibby Line (the *Devonshire*), the British India Line (the *Dilwara* and *Dunera*) and by P&O (the *Ettrick*).

The troopship *Dongola* undertook relief work at the time of the Yokohama earthquake.
Ian Allan Library

The *Assaye*, first of a class of three specialist Government troopships. She survived the longest, continuing in service until May 1928.
Ian Allan Library

Magic Nights: the *Moldavia*. ▶
Philip Rentell Collection

Merry Days: the *Moldavia* ▶
again, a postcard
celebrating a four-month
tour to Australia and New
Zealand from December
1934 to May 1935.
Philip Rentell Collection

P. & O. R.M.S. Moldavia, 16,500 Tons Gross.
Australia Mail and Passenger Service.

Launched on 25 August 1938, the *Ettrick*, like her consorts, was a twin-screw motorship of just under 12,000 gross tons equipped to carry 1,150 troops. Military accommodation was mainly in dormitory-type spaces with provision besides for 104 first-class and 90 second class passengers. With main machinery comprising two-stroke single-acting Doxford diesels, the *Ettrick* was unique as a motor-driven passenger ship in the P&O fleet of that time. She was capable of a creditable 20kt service speed.

The *Ettrick's* first voyage, a cruise in fact, to the West Indies, commenced on 16 January 1939. She was hardly able to get into her stride, though, before the outbreak of war ended all peacetime trooping and, for that matter, all luxury cruising as well as all regular service voyages. For the next six years, troop carrying was to be a serious and arduous affair. Furthermore, the ships of P&O were to be engaged in duties that would take them to more ports and to more unfamiliar parts of the ocean than ever they would have visited on numerous cruise excursions.

The *Strathaird* depicted at one of the many exotic destinations that were a feature of a P&O cruise in the 1930s.
P&O Line ▶

Towards the end of her career, the *Kaiser-I-Hind* was also employed on cruises. ▼
Philip Rentell Collection

P. & O. S.S. "KAISAR-I-HIND."
(11,518 TONS, 16,000 HORSE-POWER.)

PLEASURE CRUISES *by* P&O

BOOK HERE - NO FEE

HM Transport *Plassy*, sister-ship to the *Assaye. Maritime Photo Library*

The *Ettrick*, P&O's only diesel-powered passenger vessel over a 50-year period. She was the last to be completed of a quartet of new ships for peacetime trooping for the Ministry of Transport. *P&O Line*

5. AUXILIARY SERVICE IN THE WAR AT SEA

The large modern fleet of passenger ships constructed by P&O between 1923 and 1939 proved to be a valuable national asset in time of war. Without exception, the ships were requisitioned for auxiliary duties from the start of the war with Germany. For the most part, their size, speed and capacious bunkering space, designed for the long run from Bombay across the Indian Ocean to Australia or onwards to ports in the Far East, made them ideal for enlistment as Armed Merchant Cruisers.

Apart from the 'Strath' ships and the *Viceroy of India*, every other unit of the P&O passenger fleet was commissioned in this capacity, commencing with the *Comorin*, *Rajputana*, *Ranpura*, *Rawalpindi*, *Cathay*, *Chitral*, *Maloja*, *Mooltan* and *Ranchi* which were armed, repainted and ready to assume their new duties by October 1939. The *Canton* and *Corfu* followed in November 1939 and the *Carthage* in January 1940. Most of the conversions were carried out in Bombay.

These ships were deployed in different ocean regions established by the Admiralty for their strategic importance, some working together, but the majority far removed from the sea areas in which they had operated on peacetime schedules. The *Canton*, *Chitral*, *Corfu* and *Maloja* were attached to the Orkney and Shetlands Squadron. Placed on the East Indies station were the *Carthage*, *Cathay* and *Ranchi* while down in the South Atlantic along with Royal Mail, Union Castle and Aberdeen & Commonwealth vessels were the *Comorin*, allocated to patrol duties, and the *Mooltan* and *Ranpura* which were employed on escort work. The *Rawalpindi* and *Rajputana* were engaged on patrol work in the North Atlantic between Iceland and the Faeroes. In this capacity the *Rawalpindi* fell P&O's first victim of the war when, totally outmatched, she intercepted and engaged the German battlecruisers *Scharnhorst* and *Gneisenau* on 23 November 1939. Despite the hopelessly one-sided nature of the ensuing contest, in the finest traditions of the Royal Navy, the *Rawalpindi* turned to head straight at her adversary, having realised that escape was impossible, her small guns

firing but making little impression. After the briefest of exchanges, the *Rawalpindi* was reduced to a burning wreck, sinking with the loss of 275 lives from her reservist crew. Twenty-six survivors were captured and interned as prisoners-of-war, another 11 were picked up by the *Rawalpindi's* fleetmate *Chitral* which was patrolling in the same area.

The British Prime Minister said of the incident: 'Those men must have known as soon as they sighted the enemy that there was no chance for them, but they had no thought of surrender. Their example will be an inspiration to those who come after them.' The *Rawalpindi*, like the *Ranchi*, *Rajputana* and other vessels of the 'C' classes was not recognisable as the prewar ship of the Bombay express run, for all had lost their second funnel during the conversion into auxiliaries.

P&O's second wartime loss occurred in quite different circumstances. While patrolling in mid-Atlantic, the 16-year-old *Comorin* suffered an engine-room fire on 6 April 1941 which then spread to engulf the entire ship. For her crew it

The *Rawalpindi* in navy grey as an Armed Merchant Cruiser.
Imperial War Museum – HU993

was a nightmare, hundreds of miles from land and with no
assistance at hand. With night fast approaching, the blazing
ship stood out like a beacon, a magnet to both friend and foe
and, to make matters worse, the weather was foul, blowing a
gale and a heavy sea running. Even if help reached her,
evacuation of the *Comorin* would be difficult. Her distress
signals were, fortunately, intercepted by the Royal Navy
destroyers HMS *Broke* and HMS *Lincoln* which rushed to the
scene. There, coming alongside as best they could and by
drifting rafts and other floating apparatus towards the
afflicted *Comorin*, they were able to rescue 425 of her
complement. As it was, 20 others were killed but it could
have been far worse. As for the *Comorin*, reduced to a drifting
derelict, she was finished off the next day by a torpedo from
the *Broke*.

Just seven days later, the *Rajputana* was also sunk but in
her case by a torpedo fired by the enemy. Attacked by the
U108 to the west of Ireland, she was hit twice taking her
final plunge stern first, a sinking which cost the lives of six
of her officers and 35 ratings. Again, the death toll could
have been higher but Allied aircraft assisted rescue ships to
locate the *Rajputana*, permitting several hundred other men
to reach safety. While the rescue effort could not be
described as a triumph, it certainly prevented what would
otherwise have been a tragedy.

From around this time, the Admiralty began to release
the various P&O ships still operating as Armed Merchant
Cruisers for other duties and for the most part they were
converted to troopships. The greater numbers of regular
naval cruisers, strengthened by the many modern ships of
this type of the United States Navy which had become
available from December 1941, reduced the dependency on
the valiant vulnerable former merchant vessels. At the same
time, the tide of the war had turned favourably and the
Allies were going over to the offensive. This meant that
invasion forces had to be assembled and with them
troopships to carry the fighting men for transfer to the
beachhead.

The *Mooltan* and *Malaga* were first to make the transition,
assuming troopship duties from late 1941 after conversion at
Bombay. They had served as Armed Merchant Cruisers for

just under two years. The five 'Strath' liners and the *Viceroy of
India* had been employed in the troop-carrying role since
early in the war. They were engaged in the massive
movement of troops from Australia and New Zealand to the
Red Sea. The *Strathnaver* had been a distinctive unit of the
first big 'Down Under' convoy, sailing from Sydney on 10
January 1940 in consort with four large Orient Line ships.

Throughout 1942 and 1943, the remaining P&O vessels
underwent modification joining the ranks of troopships. By
the end of the war, with the exception of the *Ranpura* which
was purchased outright by the Admiralty for adaptation to a
Base Repair Ship, all P&O passenger vessels were being
utilised for troop-carrying work. Their contribution to the
Allies' great naval strategy helped to take the war to the
enemy in North Africa, Europe and the islands of the Pacific.
Over the course of the six-year war, P&O's fleet of troop
carriers, working for the Ministry of War Transport, conveyed
around a million fighting men to and from the battlefields.
But this effort, too, was not without its sacrifices.

For P&O, the most demanding of the amphibious operations was Operation 'Torch', the campaign to drive the Axis forces out of North Africa, involving simultaneous landings in Tunisia, Morocco and Algeria. From its beginning, on 8 November 1942, through to the dispersal of the invasion fleet late that December, the operation cost P&O and its subsidiaries more than 110,000 tons of lost shipping. P&O certainly bore the brunt of the losses for the company's ships represented 30% of the force's strength. It suffered five major losses out of the eight fleet units it contributed to the campaign.

The first victim, on 12 November, was the *Cathay* which was caught by marauding German aircraft as she was unloading troops off Bougie. She and the close-by British India Line ship *Karanja*, which sank the next day, were bombed repeatedly. At first it was thought that the *Cathay* had survived the bombardment but an unexploded bomb, which had penetrated her decks, detonated in the night, sealing her fate. Only one life was lost, the troops having been got ashore and her crew already taken off.

The once magnificent *Viceroy of India* went next, having survived the landing phase of the assault only to be hit by a torpedo fired by *U407*, as she steamed 35 miles off Oran. Empty of troops, she was on the return voyage for the invasion fleet's first wave. The destroyer HMS *Boadicea* stood by to pick up survivors before the proud *Viceroy*, which had looked splendid even in her coat of grey, sadly but spectacularly up-ended, sinking almost vertically.

The old *Narkunda*, which had somehow survived the fleet redundancies of the late 1930s, became a troopship in May 1940. She fell another victim of aircraft attack on 14 November 1942. Having already survived a torpedo attack from the Italian submarine *Platino* as she had approached the landing zone she was caught off Bougie the following evening, when bound for Algiers. Bombed by German warplanes she was left sinking with the loss of 31 lives.

Next day, the almost new peacetime troopship *Ettrick* was added to the list of casualties of Operation 'Torch', another torpedo attack accounting for her. Like the *Narkunda* and *Viceroy of India* she was caught unprotected, while returning to the River Clyde after completing her duties in association with the invasion. As she passed Azeu, 150 miles west of Gibraltar, she was hit and sunk by the submarine *U155*. Eighteen naval ratings and seven Indian crew members were killed.

All these sinkings hurt P&O as well as the national war effort, the loss of the *Viceroy of India* being perhaps the most painful up to that point, from P&O's perspective. But before the closure of the North African landings operation, P&O was to suffer an even more tragic loss, their newest ship to enter the Australian express service, the great, white *Strathallan*, which had only given them 18 months of commercial employment.

The *Strathallan* was torpedoed by *U562* on 21 December 1942, 40 miles north of Oran, as she was bound for the North African landing zone with a huge complement of replenishment forces. In total she was carrying 5,087 persons – 4,408 troops and 248 nurses plus her crew of 431. The torpedo hit set off fires in her engine room which rapidly spread in the direction of her cargo holds which were stuffed tight with ammunition. Immediate abandonment of the ship was ordered because of the risk of further explosions and all but 11 of her complement were safely removed. The *Strathallan* foundered the following morning as salvage tugs attempted to tow her to port.

No further sinkings were suffered by P&O vessels after that time, some consolation given the punishing losses of Operation 'Torch'. As it was, P&O's proud fleet of 20 passenger ships which had existed in September 1939 had been reduced to 11 by August 1945.

As with the vessels of other companies, the ships of P&O continued in their Government work long after the cessation of hostilities, repatriating the vast numbers of service personnel, refugees and other displaced persons, all the human flotsam thrown up as the ravages of war touched so many ordinary lives.

The first ship released to P&O by the Ministry of War Transport was the *Stratheden*, in July 1946. She had steamed 468,000 miles during the war, visiting Australia, India, the Middle East, South Africa, the United States, Canada and Norway. In the course of her auxiliary duties she had carried close on 150,000 troops, a record that was typical of the P&O fleet as a whole.

The *Cathay* ablaze and
sinking off the Algerian
coast on 11 November 1942,
after German aircraft
attacked her during the
Operation 'Torch' landings.
*Imperial War Museum –
A12834*

The *Strathnaver* transporting
troops in May 1942.
*Imperial War Museum –
A10613*

Sinking off the coast of
North Africa, the *Viceroy of
India*, also on 11 November
1942, another victim of the
German submarine force.
*Imperial War Museum –
HU62985*

The *Strathallan*'s brief career was ended by the torpedoes of *U562* as she arrived off the Algerian beachhead at Oran with a large contingent of reinforcements.
Alex Duncan

The end of the *Strathallan*, ablaze off Algeria after the torpedo attack in December 1942.
P&O Line

The Armed Merchant Cruiser *Corfu* off Greenock on 1 May 1943. Earlier, in July 1940, the *Corfu* was in collision with the aircraft carrier HMS *Hermes* off Freetown.
Imperial War Museum – A16365

The war is over but troop carrying continues: the *Strathmore* in Valletta Harbour, Malta on 15 February 1946.
Michael Cassar

Over a year later, on 29 August 1947, the *Chitral* seen at the same location is still engaged on repatriation duties.
Michael Cassar

The fleet repair ship HMS *Ranpura* continued in Navy service until 1961.
World Ship Naval Photo Library

6. RESUMPTION OF THE DOMINIONS AND FAR EAST SERVICES

The prospect of a full restoration of P&O's scheduled services was in the offing with the return to peacetime conditions, despite the domestic impoverishment and the much more severe losses of ships incurred during this war. P&O's misfortune had been that the company's passenger vessels were perfectly suited to the demands of auxiliary work, had been well used therefore and, as a consequence, had suffered a proportionately higher number of casualties.

The world that emerged from the bleak years of war, in 1945, was a far cry from that which had existed six years earlier – socially, politically and technologically. All these changes had to be taken into consideration in setting the direction of operational policy for the foreseeable future as well as in the planning of replacement tonnage.

In the 1920s P&O had embarked on a massive rebuilding programme comprising 12 new passenger ships. Over a similar period, following World War 2, just four new ships were ordered. Instead, a much greater emphasis was placed on fully refitting and modernising those relatively new liners, completed in the prewar years, that had survived the war. As necessary, the older vessels which were still available to P&O were placed on lower grade one-class operations pending the clearer definition of future trading patterns.

Back in 1938, Sir William Currie had taken over as Chairman of the company, following the retirement of Lord Craigmyle. It fell to the new Chairman, who had already been burdened with managing P&O's affairs during the war years, to oversee the restoration of the fleet and the schedule of sailings.

P&O's passenger services to Australia were reopened in July 1947 by the *Stratheden*, following a comprehensive, 10-month refurbishment at Barrow-in-Furness. As a

▼ The *Strathmore* together with the *Iberia*.
Ian Shiffmann

troopship she had covered nearly ½ million miles of ocean, transporting almost 150,000 troops and civilians. As restored, her passenger accommodation was reduced, some of the former cabin space having been adapted to provide improved crew quarters. She quickly settled into a regular programme of sailings which extended unbroken, apart from cruises, for the best part of the next 17 years. The only, brief interruption from this pattern was in 1950 when Cunard chartered her for a small number of Atlantic crossings on the New York run.

The other three surviving 'Strath' class ships were restored to the Sydney service via Bombay over the next three years as they too were successively decommissioned from Government auxiliary work and put through refits. The enormous demands on overstretched shipyards, exacerbated by shortages of essential materials, with commensurate delays, had more to say in determining the rate at which ships could resume their commercial schedules than anything else.

The *Strathaird* returned to commercial passenger-carrying in January 1948. She, too, had carried a large number of service personnel during her wartime career, some 130,000 in total. Next to return to the Australian service was the *Strathmore* which commenced her first postwar route voyage on 27 October 1949.

Last to be released from trooping duties was the *Strathnaver*. She was reconditioned at Belfast, re-entering the Australian trade on 5 January 1950. As restored, the *Strathnaver* and *Strathaird* had lost their dummy first and third funnels. With only a single funnel, they looked closer in appearance to the other 'Strath' pair, almost like a class of identical ships, but closer inspection revealed their many differences, one from another.

In 1954, the *Strathnaver* and *Strathaird* were downgraded, converted to one-class ships, offering accommodation space for 1,250 tourist-class passengers. Simultaneously, they omitted the Bombay call as the Indian subcontinent was by this time being more than adequately served by the faster vessels operating the route onwards to the Far East.

Perhaps the most arduous war service experienced by any of the P&O ships was that of the *Canton*. She had steamed 221,000 miles over the six years of fighting. After a full overhaul and renovation in 1946, she had the honour of re-establishing the passenger services to the Far East in October 1947, calling at Ceylon, Singapore, Malaya, Hong Kong and China although initially the route was not extended to Japan. As a recent adversary, accused of the most terrible war crimes, having subjected military and civilian prisoners of war to appalling maltreatment, it was not felt then that the conditions were right for the restoration of this link.

The *Canton* was repainted in the white livery she had first adopted in 1939 as an indication that this colour scheme was to be universally applied to the P&O fleet. However, the older vessels, like the *Mooltan*, *Maloja* and *Ranchi*, retained black hulls and funnels for the remainder of their careers.

It became possible to resume regular monthly sailings on the Far East service once the *Canton* had been rejoined by the reconditioned *Carthage* and *Corfu*. Both had been modernised to satisfy the postwar expectations of passengers travelling on this route. They were rebuilt with a single funnel. The *Corfu* had been one of the first ships to enter Singapore Harbour, after the Japanese surrender, as part of a very welcome first relief convoy. Both she and her sister ship helped in the repatriation of servicemen prior to the resumption of their commercial sailings, the *Carthage* returning to service in 1948 and the *Corfu* in 1949. On all three ships the old second-class was discarded in favour of a tourist-class grade.

P&O's oldest surviving ships, the *Mooltan* and *Maloja*, were returned to service in the summer of 1948, again following a full overhaul and refit. As converted back for passenger-carrying duties, the *Mooltan* at the Harland & Wolff shipyard, Belfast and the *Maloja* on the River Thames in London, they were turned into one-class vessels, catering for 1,030 passengers in tourist-class. Restored to the Australia route, sailing from Tilbury, the *Maloja* commenced her first postwar voyage on 10 June 1948 while the *Mooltan* rejoined her just over two months later, making her first departure on 26 August 1948. The pair maintained this tourist-only service for the next six years.

For other, older units of the P&O fleet, continued employment in the immediate postwar period saw them

The *Carthage*, a postwar view, with single funnel and white-painted hull.
Ian Allan Library

The *Maloja* returned to a one-class, tourist operation after World War 2. Her mainmast, which had been removed during the war, was not restored.
Ian Allan Library

There's a welcome 'down under' for you

Boomerang tickets to **AUSTRALIA** and back at greatly reduced cost

P&O

engaged in the revived emigrant service. Typically, emigration volumes had reflected the fluctuations of the home economy and the prospects for secure, sustainable employment, a fundamental requirement for building a decent quality of life. The rate of emigration to Australia had declined significantly in the late 1930s in the run-up to war. This was because the deteriorating political situation, no matter how threatening, had been a catalyst for a military build-up that ensured full factories and a welcome respite from the bleak dole years of the Depression. The reverse was the case after the war. Despite the prospects of healthy employment as the massive task of rebuilding the national infrastructure got underway, there was, nevertheless, a profound and widespread desire to get away from the enforced austerity, the continuing food rationing, the shortages and the evidence all around of the recent war. There was a sense that a better life could be better attained in a younger, vibrant country like Australia. Responding to the increased interest in emigration, the British and Australian Governments, through a bilateral agreement, implemented the Free and Assisted Passage Scheme on 31 March 1947, marking the beginning of large-scale postwar migration to Australia. Free passages were made available for eligible ex-servicemen and their families, assisted passages, requiring a contribution of £10 for each adult over the age of 19, were offered to all other applicants. There was no shortage of applications. By the end of 1947 they were approaching 650,000 with long queues regularly forming outside Australia House. The single limiting factor, preventing the processing of larger numbers of migrants, was the restricted availability of ships to convey the would-be settlers. P&O was intimately involved in the resettlement effort, a natural extension of its prewar participation in the emigrant trade. Two of the older passenger liners were converted for this purpose while P&O chartered additional ships for the task, primarily from the Government.

When the *Ranchi*, the only survivor of the 'R' class, was released for her postwar refit at Belfast, she was equipped to carry 950 emigrants commencing with her first sailing on 17 June 1948. She continued in the emigrant service until 1952, making her final run to Australia on 6 October that

year. Following her return to the United Kingdom, on 19 January 1953, she was disposed of for breaking up at Newport, South Wales.

Supporting the *Ranchi* and similarly converted for dedicated involvement in the Australian emigrant trade was the old *Chitral* which could cater for 740 emigrant berths in simple accommodation. From 30 December 1948, when she embarked upon her first voyage, until 1953, she supported the transportation of Australian settlers throughout the peak years without break. She was broken up at Dalmuir from April 1953.

Such was the scale of this huge population movement, engaging the vessels of Shaw-Savill as well as P&O Line, that additional tonnage was required. This was satisfied by the employment of a range of Government-owned carriers, British ships that for one reason or another had not been returned to their original owners or captured foreign vessels which had been pressed into troop-carrying work and which, therefore, offered accommodation adequate for subsidised emigrant passages. For a short period, P&O chartered the former Cunard White Star motorship *Georgic*, later managing her on behalf of the Australian Government during a second spell of emigrant transportation. As the 1950s wore on and shipping matters in general settled down, simultaneous with a levelling of demand for assisted passages, the carriage of these passengers was once again satisfied by the allocation of sections of cabin space aboard the liners running the scheduled services.

These were not the most glamorous years for P&O, compelled to do the best it could in difficult circumstances.

Launched on 5 October 1948 by Lady Currie, wife of Sir William Currie, the P&O Chairman, the *Himalaya* takes to the water watched by workmen in the foreground.
Ian Allan Library

Close-up view of the *Himalaya's* upper deck and funnel during her trials, on 1 September 1949. Note that only men can be seen on deck – no doubt, all shipyard employees.
Ian Allan Library

◄ The completed *Himalaya*, a general view. A Thornycroft smoke clearance extension was later added to her funnel.
Tom Rayner Collection

▲ Similar to the *Himalaya*, but smaller, the *Chusan* entered service on 1 July 1950.
Ian Allan Library

Hold-ups in the shipbuilding yards, complicated by increasing costs as demand outstripped supply, were impacting on the entry into service of new ships under construction and delaying orders for additional vessels. Though fully overhauled and refurnished, the older vessels on the Australia, India and Far East runs were having to operate at faster speeds and, to some extent, carrying a greater capacity of passengers than was desirable. The 'Straths' schedule was tightened-up in such a way that each vessel made four rather than three round voyages each year. But all this was about to change. P&O had ordered its first new passenger liner of the postwar period back in the spring of 1946, one of the ships that had been caught up in the shipyard problems. When she finally emerged, late in 1949, she was splendid, the largest and fastest ship the company had ever owned, with a gross tonnage of around 28,000 tons

and having achieved a creditable 25kt speed on her builder's trials. Christened *Himalaya* when launched on 5 October 1948 by Lady Currie, the wife of the P&O Chairman, she perpetuated a name which was closely linked with the company's successful traditions and she proved to be no exception to this, as her achievements were to demonstrate. Her maiden voyage from Tilbury to Sydney via Bombay and Melbourne took place on 6 October 1949.

The *Himalaya* had been constructed at Barrow alongside Orient Line's similar-sized *Orcades*, marking a gradual coming together of the design and style of the new liners of either company. That said, whereas the dimensions of the two ships were broadly the same, the *Himalaya* retained a more orthodox appearance, her only concession to modernity, externally, being the absence of a mainmast. She was turbine-driven with twin screws and had accommodation for

With Table Mountain behind her, the rebuilt *Strathnaver* calls at Cape Town. The *Strathnaver* represented P&O at the Coronation Fleet Review in 1953. *Ian Allan Library*

The *Strathaird* also seen during a visit to Table Bay. During their postwar refits, the *Strathaird* and *Strathnaver* lost their dummy first and third funnels. *Ian Allan Library*

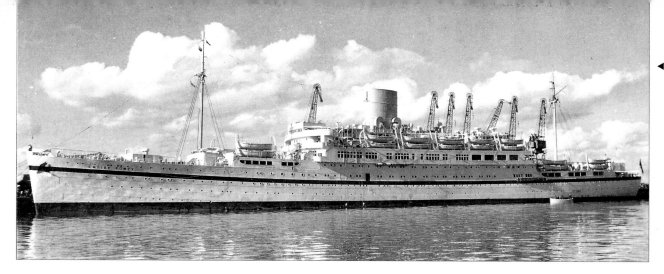

1,160 passengers in two classes. Her cargo spaces included 235,000cu ft of capacity for refrigerated produce.

Being capable of much higher speeds than previous vessels on the Australian run, the *Himalaya* was also a record breaker, eclipsing the best times on all stages of the route. She cut the United Kingdom to Bombay passage by five days and reduced the overall voyage time to Australia from 38 days to 28 days!

This level of performance proved invaluable for both her and her later consorts, when from November 1956 the Suez Canal was closed. The shorter route via the Mediterranean was, by that time, an integral part of P&O's routes to Australia and the Far East, critical to the maintenance of schedules. Using the Canal saved 1,200 miles on the route to Australia and the East, equivalent to three to four days' steaming for a 15kt vessel. Its closure threatened major disruption. The faster speeds of the new express mail ships helped to alleviate the difficulties that resulted from enforced rerouting via the Cape.

Almost simultaneous with the *Himalaya* and in many respects like a smaller version, P&O took delivery of the new *Chusan* in July 1950, the principal element in the postwar regeneration of the Indian and Far East market.

Essentially she was the belated replacement for the *Viceroy of India* and like her celebrated predecessor she introduced superior standards on the route to the Orient. Launched on 29 June 1949, she entered service on 14 July 1950 making three luxury cruises from Southampton prior to her first line voyage from London to Bombay and return in September of the same year. Thereafter she continued to China, working with the *Corfu*, *Carthage* and *Canton*. From November 1950, she reinstated the route to Japan, making P&O's first postwar call at Yokohama.

Designed specially for the India and China services, the *Chusan* could accommodate 474 first-class and 543 tourist-class passengers. Her modern interiors, featuring extensive public spaces, occupied seven decks and, like the *Himalaya*, her large hold capacity allowed her to carry refrigerated foodstuffs as well as other cargo.

In 1951, to help keep funnel emissions away from the open passenger decks, the *Chusan* was fitted with a fluted funnel extension, specially designed by Thornycroft's of Southampton. The *Himalaya's* funnel was adapted in similar fashion around the same time.

P&O's intention of upgrading the Australia services with three vessels of the *Himalaya* type had fallen rather behind programme but were finally fulfilled in 1954 with the introduction of the *Arcadia* and *Iberia*. This spelt the end for

the *Mooltan* and *Maloja*, by now known as the 'Faithful Sisters', and they were sent for scrap, surplus to requirements, the former at Faslane in January 1954 and the latter at Inverkeithing a month later.

Bigger overall than the *Himalaya*, at almost 30,000 gross tons, but otherwise alike in terms of layout, accommodation and speed, the *Arcadia* and *Iberia* were launched respectively on 14 May 1953 at John Brown's Yard on Clydebank and 21 January 1954 at Harland & Wolff, Belfast. The *Arcadia* commenced her maiden voyage from London to Bombay, Colombo, Melbourne and Sydney on 22 February 1954. She carried 679 first-class and 735 tourist-class passengers. The *Iberia's* numbers were broadly the same, with rather more in first-class and correspondingly fewer in tourist. Along with the *Himalaya*, these P&O liners had been paralleled by three nearly equivalent Orient ships, the *Orcades*, *Oronsay* and *Orsova*. The six ships worked closer and closer together, their sailing schedules organised so that sailings alternated between P&O and Orient.

For their interior designs, P&O adhered very much to traditional concepts, avoiding jazzy over-modern patterns, but exploiting contemporary materials and modern decoration techniques to deliver a balanced, pleasing combination. Lighting, furnishing and panelling all exhibited these characteristics, giving a generally relaxed and gentle ambience to the cabins and public rooms.

With the commissioning of the *Arcadia* and *Iberia*, the P&O fleet comprised 11 beautiful white liners, seven working the Australian services and four on the India and Far East routes, plus the single troopship *Empire Fowey* managed on behalf of the Government (formerly Norddeutscher Lloyd's *Potsdam*, having been ceded to Great Britain in 1945). After a full conversion, including re-engining and reboilering, she had entered service as the *Empire Jewel*, later renamed *Empire Fowey*.

Throughout the relatively settled years of the late 1950s these ships maintained the company's services, adding to P&O's glorious reputation and building its prosperity. But the peak had not yet been reached, for even greater accomplishments were to follow in the next few years.

When the *Arcadia* entered
service in February 1954,
the standards of service and
accommodation offered by
P&O made another major
advance.
Ian Allan Library

The *Iberia*, second new liner
of the mid-1950s, made her
maiden voyage on
28 September 1954.
Ian Allan Library

7. MERGER AND SUPERLINERS

Throughout the 1950s, P&O and the Orient Line had been moving their passenger operations to Australia closer together. This was reflected in the general matching of size and capability of each company's new buildings, a prerequisite to organising balanced schedules around both fleets of ships.

From 20 January 1958 the route to Australia was extended across the Pacific Ocean in a joint service marketed under the name Orient & Pacific Line. The *Himalaya* inaugurated the operation, continuing from Sydney to Auckland, Suva, Honolulu, Vancouver and terminating at San Francisco from where the route was run in reverse. By combining the front-line steamers of both P&O and Orient into a kind of Southern Dominions 'Big Six' – the *Himalaya,*

Arcadia, Iberia, and *Orcades, Oronsay* and *Orsova* – it was possible to maintain this trade. It compensated too, for some of the reduced traffic on the United Kingdom to Australia leg, creamed off by aircraft, for which both lines were competing against each other and which resulted in all ships making the run half empty.

Hinting at a full amalgamation, the inevitable finally occurred just over two years later when on 2 May 1960, P&O—Orient Lines (Passenger Services) was formed as a single entity to manage the combined fleets of passenger liners. At the same time the name Orient & Pacific Line, which had never proved to be popular, was dropped. The merger of the two companies, the most dominant of the lines operating the Australian services, was reminiscent of

The *Iberia* early in her career.
Tom Rayner Collection

A striking bow view of the *Arcadia.*
P&O Line

the amalgamation between the Cunard and White Star Lines just 25 years earlier. For all practical purposes, Cunard, the more powerful concern, had then taken over White Star in all but name, the majority of the White Star ships being discarded and ultimately the White Star identity disappearing altogether. So it was with P&O and the Orient Line. Considering that P&O had held a dominant stake in Orient for over 40 years no other outcome was realistically in prospect. Notably the Orient Line ships were repainted in P&O white although as a minor and temporary concession they retained their green boot-topping, the Orient Line shade.

Orient's contribution to the combined fleet included their three superb front-line ships, the eldest being the 1948-built *Orcades*. The similar-sized *Oronsay* had made her maiden voyage to Sydney and Auckland on 16 May 1951, delayed through an outbreak of fire while she was fitting out. The larger *Orsova*, a contemporary to P&O's *Arcadia* and *Iberia*, completed the trio. She had made her début on the Australia run on 17 March 1954. Apart from their distinctive colouring, the three liners were outstanding for having 'Welsh Hat' funnel tops, as they were described, black cowls with pipe extensions. The *Orsova*, as a one-off, could also boast another unusual feature, having no navigational masts whatsoever.

So the fleet was swollen by the addition of the five Orient Line ships: the *Orcades*, *Oronsay* and *Orsova* plus the older *Orion*, built in the 1930s and the veteran two-funneller *Orontes*. The latter two ships were disposed of within three years along with the four remaining 'Strath' ships.

From the time of the introduction of the new *Arcadia* and *Iberia*, the *Strathnaver* and *Strathaird* had been converted to single-class tourist ships, adding 200 more berths to their accommodation. However, following the emigration boom of the late 1940s and early 1950s, the emigrant trade had declined somewhat although it briefly flourished again between 1956 and 1960, no doubt fuelled by anxieties aroused by the Suez and Hungarian crises. Demand having fallen off yet again, P&O considered that the older 'Strath' pair could be retired, leaving the *Strathmore* and *Strathallan*, which by then had also been converted into one-class vessels, to sustain this business.

Arriving at Vancouver,
the *Arcadia*.
Ian Shiffmann

Run away to sea!

P&O
WORLD WIDE SERVICES

Both the *Strathaird* and the *Strathnaver* were sold for breaking up at Hong Kong, the former from July 1961 and the latter just under a year later. Ironically, just 12 months on, the demand for sponsored passages to Australia and New Zealand was to rise again quite unexpectedly, a consequence, it might be speculated, of one of the longest and coldest British winters on record.

At the time when the P&O and Orient Lines merged, both companies also had a single large new liner under construction, each conceived with the trans-Pacific service in mind, the fabrication of the Orient vessel being the more advanced of the two. They were to be the crowning glory of almost a century and a quarter of passenger services to Australasia, the largest and most magnificent vessels ever placed on the route by any line of any nationality. Equally, they were both very ambitious ships, radically different in appearance though bearing no resemblance to each other, each representing a bold design statement.

On reflection, it may seem to have been poor business judgement bringing out such large ships at a time when the encroachment into the passenger trade by aircraft was gaining ground. The fact was though, that the longer routes to Australia, the Far East and across the Pacific had not yet been undermined by airline travel to the same extent as the relatively short, more heavily patronised North Atlantic crossing. The new-generation jet airliners did not yet have

◄ The **P&O poster 'Run Away to Sea'** was a reissue of an Orient Line original first published in 1958 and later revamped, with a slightly different photograph, for P&O-Orient Lines.
P&O Line

▲ The *Iberia* as completed.
Ian Shiffmann

The *Chusan*, a photograph taken in 1952.
Maritime Photo Library

The *Iberia* again, seen in the Solent, passing the Isle of Wight. For some unexplained reason she was not as successful as her older sister. She was one of the first of P&O's new postwar scheduled service liners to be disposed of for scrap.
Ian Allan Library

The *Canberra* taking shape at Belfast in November 1959. Extensive use was made of aluminium in the construction of her superstructure.
Ian Allan Library

3264

the capacity, range or fuel efficiency required to seriously challenge the ships on the run to the Orient or the Southern Dominions. This would happen later, as the 1960s advanced.

Ironically, back in 1955, P&O had itself toyed with the idea of adopting aircraft in place of ships for its primary passenger routes. It engaged the flying boat constructors Saunders-Roe to carry out a feasibility study into a massive, 1,000-passenger jet-engined superplane. This extraordinary marine aircraft, which would have dwarfed the Boeing 747 and which could have cut the London to Sydney passage time from 28 days to around four days maximum, never materialised, although it was said to be absolutely viable. P&O, for all its greater willingness to adapt and lead the way, was not prepared to be that revolutionary!

By 1956, the Suez Canal had been dredged and widened sufficiently to allow ships as large as 40,000 gross tons to make passage through the waterway. Accordingly, both P&O and Orient specified vessels of this size in their new liner contracts.

The Orient ship, the *Oriana*, constructed by Vickers Armstrong at Barrow-in-Furness, made her first line voyage on 3 December 1960 on the London to San Francisco route via Australia. She had been launched on 3 November 1959, entering service in November 1960 with a cruise from Southampton to Lisbon during the course of which the Association of British Travel Agents held its annual convention on board.

Of the two superliners, the *Oriana* was the more conventional but she was striking nevertheless. Her attractive lines featured a gradual build-up of her decks to the centre of the ship, upon which two unequally-sized and stepped funnel structures were erected. Completed in the distinctive corn-coloured hull of the Orient Line, which she continued to wear for the next four years, it has to be said that she looked significantly better in this livery than ever she did in the P&O white hull colours. The *Oriana* was superbly appointed, the quality of her cabin accommodation, public rooms and on-board facilities being of the highest order for all classes of her 1,500 complement of passengers. She was steam turbine-powered, driving twin screws, giving

a service speed of 23kt which cut the passage time out to Australia still further.

Meanwhile, the slightly larger but equally dramatic new P&O flagship *Canberra* was taking shape at the Belfast shipyard of Harland & Wolff. If the *Oriana* represented something of a departure from earlier Orient Line design considerations then, measured by the same standards, the *Canberra* was a complete break from established P&O tradition.

She reverted to turbo-electric machinery, after an interruption of almost 30 years, but in her case the engine installation was placed back aft, permitting unprecedented freedom to the designers in the layout and fabrication of passenger accommodation in the forward areas of the ship.

Thus, room after room, feature after feature was linked together without interference from either service trunking or the uptakes of boiler flues. This distribution of facilities afforded other benefits too, resolving issues that had for long tested the ingenuity of marine engineers and naval architects.

Placing the engines at the stern kept engine noise away from the majority of the cabin spaces, greatly improving passenger comfort. Equally, on deck, the nuisance of smoke smuts was eliminated at a stroke, the twin side-by-side, gracefully curved funnels exhausting away over the stern, clear of even the recreation and promenade areas located at the stern. Just as with her interiors, the vast uninterrupted deck spaces were exploited to the full in the provision of

Seen from the air, the *Chusan* **off Sydney Heads.** *Ian Shiffmann*

The *Oronsay* **at Durban after repainting in P&O colours.** *Ian Shiffmann*

In her original corn-coloured livery, the *Oronsay*, one of the five Orient Line ships to be absorbed into the joint P&O-Orient fleet.
Tom Rayner Collection

The first super-liner built for the Australia service and the largest vessel ever owned by Orient Line, the *Oriana* on acceptance trials.
Vickers Limited

The *Orsova*, third of Orient Line's postwar trio of large express liners for the Australia mail run.
Ian Shiffmann

The P&O Orient fleet of the early 1960s – 11 ships built for the sun.
Ian Allan Library

passenger amenities. The *Canberra* was technically advanced in many ways, being, for instance, one of the first liners to have an alternating current electrical supply rather than direct current.

The shipping press of the day, rather negatively, was full of reports about flaws in the design and construction of the *Canberra*. They pointed out that model tests had not made sufficient compensation for the weight of her machinery and that, to bring her into level trim, it had been necessary to pour tons of concrete into the forward part of the hull, increasing her overall draught by 3-4ft. But all this was of no consequence. It may well have added to her operating costs, pushing deadweight around the oceans, but it certainly did

not adversely affect her popularity or limit her operational scope. Even later, as a full-time cruise liner, she followed itineraries that took her without difficulty to many small harbours and anchorages, a far cry from the vast deep-water ports of her line voyages.

The *Canberra* was launched on 16 March 1960 and entered service the following year, commencing her maiden voyage from Southampton to Colombo, Melbourne and Sydney on 2 June 1961. She attracted great interest and a keen following, the crowds gathered to see her off being reminiscent of the numbers that had earlier bade 'Bon Voyage and God Speed' to the Cunard '*Queens*'. With the *Oriana*, the *Canberra* continued on the Australia, New Zealand

and trans-Pacific service which, from time to time, became a full circumnavigation when they returned to Southampton through the Panama Canal.

At about this time, P&O acquired two smart, modern cargo passenger ships from the Belgian Company, Compagnie Maritime Belge, for operation on the Far East services. Renamed *Cathay* and *Chitral*, they replaced the *Carthage* and *Corfu* on this route which were retired in February 1961 and broken up in Japan. The new vessels carried just 274 first-class passengers, some 100 fewer berths than the outgoing pair whose accommodation had also been distributed across two grades. The *Chitral's* first P&O voyage was made in March 1961, the *Cathay's* the month after.

Retirements of older P&O vessels continued apace during this period, the *Canton* joining the parade to the block in October 1962. The company's commitment to Government trooping was also terminated when the *Empire Fowey* was sold for further trading as a pilgrim carrier under the Pakistani flag. In 1963, the *Strathmore*, on 20 June, and the *Stratheden*, on 7 August, made their final voyages to Australia. For a time the *Stratheden* was briefly chartered for cruise work after which they were sold jointly to a Greek concern, also entering the Moslem pilgrimage run from Karachi to Mecca, Saudi Arabia.

Associated with these disposals, other changes took place as P&O completed a full reorganisation of its services. The *Himalaya* was converted into a one-class ship for the Australia run. Simultaneously, the *Arcadia* and *Iberia* were extensively modernised. Air conditioning was fitted throughout both ships and they also had stabilisers installed. After a period which was spent primarily operating cruises, the *Chusan* was placed on a new regular service linking Australia and Yokohama, with a call at Hong Kong. It seemed that certain of these measures were of a temporary, even transient nature but the P&O board would have rightly argued that all its vessels were gainfully employed, continuing to earn reasonably healthy revenues. The passenger fleet, now comprising 11 vessels, was modern and well suited to flexible trading patterns, and the company as a whole was well placed to adapt to whatever the future passenger shipping business held in prospect.

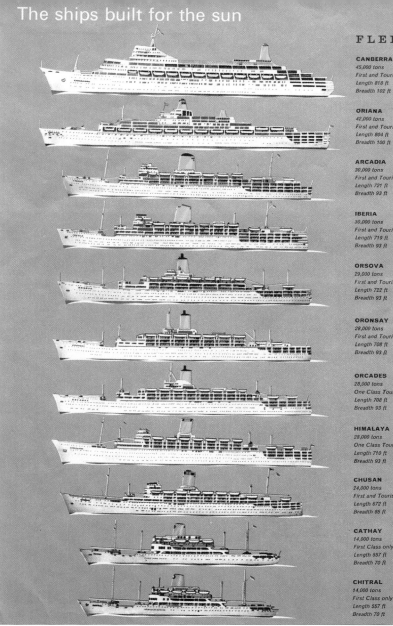

The ships built for the sun

FLEET

CANBERRA
45,000 tons
First and Tourist Class
Length 818 ft
Breadth 102 ft

ORIANA
42,000 tons
First and Tourist Class
Length 804 ft
Breadth 100 ft

ARCADIA
30,000 tons
First and Tourist Class
Length 721 ft
Breadth 93 ft

IBERIA
30,000 tons
First and Tourist Class
Length 719 ft
Breadth 93 ft

ORSOVA
29,000 tons
First and Tourist Class
Length 722 ft
Breadth 93 ft

ORONSAY
28,000 tons
First and Tourist Class
Length 708 ft
Breadth 93 ft

ORCADES
28,000 tons
One Class Tourist
Length 708 ft
Breadth 93 ft

HIMALAYA
28,000 tons
One Class Tourist
Length 710 ft
Breadth 93 ft

CHUSAN
24,000 tons
First and Tourist Class
Length 672 ft
Breadth 85 ft

CATHAY
14,000 tons
First Class only
Length 557 ft
Breadth 70 ft

CHITRAL
14,000 tons
First Class only
Length 557 ft
Breadth 70 ft

A superb view of the *Canberra* on her builder's trials. She was the largest British liner to be built since the *Queen Elizabeth*. *P&O Line*

Replacements for the old *Corfu* and *Carthage*, the former Belgian cargo passenger liners, the *Cathay*...
Ian Shiffmann

...and the *Chitral*.
Ian Shiffmann

The *Chitral* ex-*Jadotville*.
Alex Duncan

The identical *Cathay* ex-*Baudouinville*. These ships offered exclusive one-class accommodation on the service to the Far East.
Alex Duncan

This aerial view of the *Canberra* clearly reveals her remarkable layout – engines aft, large amidships recreation area and lifeboats stowed partially enclosed, low down on the promenade deck.
David L. Williams Collection

The *Canberra* berthed at Sydney, her southern terminus.
Ian Allan Library

As soon as operational conditions permitted, P&O reintroduced an annual programme of cruises to complement its roster of line voyages, altogether an unrivalled breadth of services. Most of the front-line ships in some way contributed to this activity but it was not until the late 1950s that P&O commenced any sort of reorganisation of its schedules so as to commit certain vessels to this work either full-time or even substantively.

In 1959, the *Chusan* was taken off the Far East route and extensively overhauled in readiness for operating world cruises and other long duration excursions. In her first full cruise season she undertook P&O's first global circumnavigation, a voyage of some 80 or so days' duration, covering a distance of 32,000 miles with calls at no fewer than 24 ports. At this time, the cruise programmes of the *Arcadia* and *Iberia* were increased with tours out of San Francisco along the American west coast. Apart from this,

the only other cruising of any intensity engaged the old *Strathmore* and *Stratheden* in the months prior to their retirement when they were chartered to the Travel Savings Association for a series of cruises from the summer of 1963 through into 1964.

The fact was that P&O had no need to employ its vessels more extensively cruising, certainly not then at least. Quite apart from the relative absence of serious inroads into their traditional areas of operation by aircraft at that time, a major upsurge in emigration to Australia proved to be a very useful boost to the P&O passenger shipping business through almost to the end of the decade. These turned out to be the peak years for emigration 'Down Under', surpassing by a considerable margin the total volume of emigrant traffic of the previous 15 years which itself had been swollen by the 'Bring out a Briton' campaign launched in 1957. Between 1947 and the summer of 1962, P&O and other companies

The *Iberia* at Cape Town. She too had her mainmast removed.
Ian Shiffmann

had transported 427,938 migrants but over the following eight years another 506,639 persons travelling under the provisions of the assisted emigration schemes were conveyed to Australia. Increasingly, however, airline travel was adopted for these passages as it became cheaper than the ocean voyage. The trade once more tapered off from 1970 but looking back with the value of hindsight, it had provided a valuable breathing space for P&O at a critical time in its affairs.

Sir William Currie had retired as the P&O Chairman in March 1960 after 22 years in the office, including the difficult interlude of the war years. He was followed at the helm by Sir Donald Anderson to whom was to fall the task of steering the company's fortunes through probably the most turbulent decade ever, as major changes began to sweep through the shipping industry. On the one hand traditional activities were contracting rapidly while on the

The *Arcadia* sails from Cape Town. ▼
Ian Shiffmann

'Sunshine Cruising by ▶
P&O-Orient', a poster from
1960. *P&O Line*

P&O-ORIENT SUNSHINE CRUISING

The one holiday that has everything

other, not that it was fully appreciated at the time, there were immense opportunities emerging for future development and expansion. And all this was taking place against a backdrop of economic uncertainty and worldwide political upheaval.

In 1965 P&O completed its acquisition of the Orient Steam Navigation Company, purchasing the remaining minority shareholdings to make it a wholly-owned subsidiary. Already, on 21 September 1962, the *Orcades* and *Oronsay* had been transferred into P&O ownership. From 31 March 1965, they were joined by the *Orsova* and *Oriana* when they too were reregistered as P&O ships. All four had been repainted in P&O colours in 1964. The last vestiges of Orient finally disappeared from October 1966 when the operating name P&O-Orient Line Limited was dropped in favour of P&O Line. It was the end for a famous British shipping line whose history could be traced back to the end of the 18th century. Orient Line had operated on the Australian run since 1866 as a carrier renowned for the quality of its service and excellence of its ships. It had been a trailblazer, too, in the cruise trade. Orient had been intrinsically linked with P&O since 1919, now its heritage was fully intertwined with the parent concern contributing to the totality of its glorious record.

The P&O Line had 11 passenger ships still maintaining virtually all of the same liner routes that it had been running back in 1920, plus the new trans-Pacific run. But the company could not avoid the inevitable for much longer for, whatever it did, the days of scheduled steamship services were numbered. For all its glorious past up to that time, whether or not P&O was to have a future in the ocean passenger trade would largely depend on the board's handling of the vital process of transition on which it was soon to embark. This would involve conversion into an exclusive cruise operator, the only alternative being to cease trading altogether, a position many another long-enduring passenger operator was forced into.

Ironically, in 1963, after four yea's making world cruises, the *Chusan* had been returned to a scheduled operation, plying the route from Australia to Hong Kong and Yokohama.

To a considerable extent industrial strife and international politics conspired to dramatically influence the course of events within just a few years.

First, on the home-front, P&O was badly hit when the National Union of Seamen called for an industry-wide strike commencing on 16 May 1966. All round the country, vessels of every description were laid up idle, with perhaps the huge concentrations of larger passenger ships at Southampton and London most emphatically conveying the magnitude of the stoppage. It lasted until 1 July that year, just over six weeks, but in that time a great deal of irreparable damage had been inflicted. Just as with motorway traffic jams, where road vehicles take longer to gather speed than they take to slow down, so the reactivation of strike-bound vessels was a long-winded affair. Some ships could not be mobilised again until the following March. In that length of time frame many passengers, the very consumers on whom P&O and other lines depended for their livelihoods, had made choices about how they proposed to travel in the future and it would no longer be by ship.

P&O had hardly recovered from the seamen's strike when, following the sequestration and nationalisation of the Suez Canal by Egypt, the tensions of the Middle East deteriorated into open conflict in the 'Six Day War' with Israel. In part as a consequence of the fighting across the Canal Zone but as much to do with deliberately interrupting the shipping routes upon which Israel's allies and friends depended, the Suez Canal was obstructed with sunken ships on 5 June 1967. It remained closed for the next eight years. On the plus side, if there was such a thing in a situation as negative as this, at least no P&O ships had been trapped within the closed waterway. It had been a near thing, though, for within 24hr of the closure, the *Canberra*, carrying almost a full complement of 2,200 odd passengers, was somewhat less steaming distance from what would have been an unavoidable, unwelcome and probably fatal incarceration. Luckily she was rerouted in good time, extending considerably the duration of her voyage to the United Kingdom but nevertheless subjecting her passengers to less inconvenience than they might otherwise have experienced.

Arising from the inaccessibility of the Mediterranean routes through the continued closure of the Suez Canal, P&O was compelled to reduce its dependence on the shorter sea-lanes to the Orient and Pacific. Thus the decision was made to terminate all the remaining Far East passenger services from 1969, ending over 100 years of almost unbroken operation on these routes.

As the pace of enforced change accelerated, other scheduled operations also fell victim to the cuts, each constituting a regrettable milestone in the winding down of what had for long been the company's core business, the very trade in which its glorious heritage had been assimilated. The *Chusan* ran the last ever passenger voyage to India, leaving London on 15 September 1970. The closure of this service turned out to be her swansong for within three years she too would be gone, broken up in Taiwan. Prior to their final disposal, the *Cathay* and *Chitral* were transferred from October 1970 to the Eastern & Australian Steamship Company, a British India Line subsidiary, for service between Australia and Japan.

The piecemeal demolition of the affairs of a once-proud shipping line, as seemed to be happening to P&O, can be a matter for circumspection and sad reflection but great business organisations are nothing if not resilient, able to adapt to the vagaries of commercial circumstances. P&O could have faltered at an important hurdle, caught-out trying to perpetuate its fast-disappearing, redundant past. Instead it looked forward, prepared to face the challenges of the future. That is not to say that, for a time at least, consideration was not given to abandoning the passenger

The *Arcadia* in the 1960s with her mainmast removed. She remained a popular ship on line voyages and cruises alike. *P&O Line*

shipping trade altogether. After all, P&O also had healthy bulk shipping, container cargo and short sea ferry operations to sustain it. But P&O was not ready to withdraw from this important business which was central to its very existence. It had been one of the most successful lines operating one form of passenger shipping; it would achieve equal prestige in another, if somewhat different, form.

Instead, P&O set itself a strategy by which it sought to expand rapidly into the lucrative American cruise market, exploiting the enormous potential that existed on the Pacific coast by offering excursions north to Alaska and south to Mexico. Building on the platform established some time earlier with the *Arcadia* and *Iberia*, soon all the remaining passenger ships were working in this area, when they were not running the rather fewer cruise voyages made from Southampton.

An incident in 1969, when an outbreak of typhoid occurred aboard the *Oronsay*, served to drive home another important message to P&O. The expectations of cruise passengers, particularly the discerning American traveller, were very high indeed and it was evident that, despite P&O's considerable efforts, the older vessels fell short of the desired standard. Adapting old ships was ultimately an uneconomical process giving only a temporary gain, besides which, for all the money invested, the end result was not guaranteed to achieve what was required. It had been an acceptable interim measure but the grand old ladies of the 'O' class, the *Arcadia*, *Himalaya* and *Iberia* all belonged to a different time, designed for a different job and it was time for them to make way for a new generation.

From 1972 onwards, P&O progressively invested in new, purpose-built, state-of-the-art cruise ships, the first being

The *Oronsay* with P&O white hull. She commenced her maiden voyage on 16 May 1973.
Ian Allan Library

The *Chusan* did not survive P&O's transition into an exclusive cruise operator. She survived until June 1973.
Ian Allan Library

The most conspicuous feature of the *Orsova* was the total absence of masts. Here she is painted in P&O colours.
Ian Allan Library

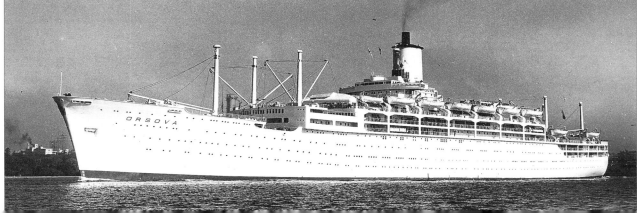

Another striking view of the *Arcadia*. Before she was disposed of in 1979 she became a full-time cruise liner.
P&O Line

The *Canberra* in the English Channel. In the distance beyond her is the Norddeutscher Lloyd liner *Berlin*. The *Canberra* experienced an on-board fire off Italy on 4 January 1963 which left her main engines out of action. The old *Stratheden* went to her assistance. Rather than causing her to suffer from bad publicity, the incident was handled so professionally that P&O's image was elevated in the estimation of many passengers.
Ian Allan Library

the relatively small *Spirit of London* purchased on the stocks while building for the Norwegian-flag Lauritz Kloster concern. As for the old vessels, within a very few years they had gone completely – the *Iberia* scrapped in 1972, the *Orcades*, *Orsova* and *Himalaya* in 1974, and the *Oronsay* in 1975. Only the *Arcadia* lasted longer, pending the arrival of new vessels.

Removing this many ships in quick succession threatened to leave a vacuum in the American west coast cruise trade which would be filled by competitors. To offset this and to maintain the position P&O had already established, the 10-year-old Princess Cruises company was acquired in October 1974, specifically for this sector. Its two modern ships, *Pacific Princess* and *Island Princess* were supplemented

by the existing *Spirit of London*, suitably renamed *Sun Princess*, the trio inaugurating the now legendary 'Love Boat' cruise operation complete with its own TV series.

The *Oriana* and *Canberra* did not succeed as cruise ships on the American circuit even though they were much newer and had more modern appointments. Their size, and the cost of running such large ships, combined with the associated expense of carrying out any major internal renovation placed them at risk. Since the dues for the transit of the Panama Canal had also been increased the round-the-world run via the Pacific Ocean had been ended and no other employment appeared to be available for them. To the credit of P&O, backed up by some persuasive advertising, niche markets were carved out for both ships, operating cruises from the

◀◀ An overhead view of the *Oriana* taken from Vancouver Bridge.
Ian Shiffmann

▼ The specially built cruise ship *Spirit of London* was small by comparison to the giant cruise vessels which would be introduced by P&O within 30 years as its cruise operation expanded and grew.
Ian Shiffmann

An imposing view of the *Oriana*. She was involved in an accident early in her career when she collided with the United States' aircraft carrier USS *Kearsage* in December 1962.
Ian Allan Library

The purpose-built *Spirit of London*, P&O's first pure cruise ship.
Alex Duncan

◀ The *Canberra* at the time of her proudest achievement, departing Southampton at night to join the South Atlantic Task Force at the time of the Falklands War. *Southern Daily Echo*

▼ The *Canberra's* glorious return from the Falklands. The 'great white whale' was hardly the most flattering sobriquet for her, conjuring up images of Herman Melville's vengeful leviathan. In fact, she was the most elegant of P&O's long line of beautiful white liners. *Peter A. Alford*

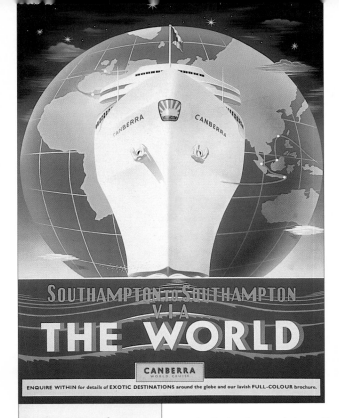

▲ United Kingdom and Australia and, in the fullness of time, they became two of P&O's most successful and best earning cruise ships.

P&O's full transition from scheduled service provider to cruise voyage operator took about 10 years to complete. Beyond that, as the company forged for itself a new era of achievement, was the glorious participation in the South
▶ Atlantic Task Force at the time of the campaign to recover the invaded Falkland Islands, notably the contribution of the *Canberra*.

Fifteen years further on, P&O had become one of the leading cruise ship operators as the boom in this type of holiday was set to continue on through the end of the millennium. The careers of the *Canberra* and *Oriana*

eventually ended, their passing occasioning by a certain poignancy, but in their place an immense fleet of specialist cruise ships had come into being, sailing under the banners of P&O Cruises and Princess Cruises. Amazingly, as it would no doubt have seemed if suggested back in 1970, P&O was to run passenger ships under the Princess banner which could briefly claim to be the largest ever built, in tonnage terms far bigger even than the old Cunard 'Queen' liners.

No doubt, too, P&O will continue as a force in cruise shipping in the 21st century. Who knows what other developments will arise as this burgeoning trade continues to open up new possibilities but one thing for certain is that P&O, in keeping with its glorious traditions, will be a part of them.

Naldera (1920-38)
Caird & Co, Greenock, launched 29 December 1917.
16,088grt; 605ft loa.
Passengers: 426-first, 247-second.
Crew: 462.
Engines: quadruple expansion steam reciprocating, 18,000ihp; twin screw, 17kt.
Fate: broken up at Bo'ness, Firth of Forth, November 1938.

Narkunda (1920-42)
Harland & Wolff, Belfast, launched 25 April 1918.
16,118grt; 606ft loa.
Passengers: 426-first, 247-second.
Crew: 462.
Engines: quadruple expansion steam reciprocating, 18,000ihp; twin screw, 17kt.
Fate: bombed and sunk off Bougie, Algeria, 14 November 1942.

Baradine (1921-36)
Harland & Wolff, Belfast, launched 27 November 1920.
13,144grt; 537ft loa.
Passengers: 491-third plus 743 temporary steerage berths.
Crew: 288.
Engines: quadruple expansion steam reciprocating, 9,500ihp (exhaust steam turbines added 1929, 12,000ihp); twin screw, 15kt.
Fate: broken up at Dalmuir, June 1936.

Ballarat (1922-35)
Harland & Wolff, Greenock, launched 14 September 1920.
13,065grt; 537ft loa.
Passengers: 491-third plus 743 temporary steerage berths.
Crew: 288.
Engines: quadruple expansion steam reciprocating, 9,500ihp (exhaust steam turbines added 1929, 12,000ihp); twin screw, 15kt.
Fate: broken up at Briton Ferry, South Wales, May 1935

Balranald (1922-36)
Harland & Wolff, Greenock, launched 24 February 1921.
13,039grt; 537ft loa.
Passengers: 491-third plus 743 temporary steerage berths.
Crew: 288.
Engines: quadruple expansion steam reciprocating, 9,500ihp (exhaust steam turbines added 1929, 12,000ihp); twin screw, 15kt.
Fate: broken up at Troon, 1936.

Bendigo (1922-36)
Harland & Wolff, Greenock, launched 26 January 1922.
13,039grt; 537ft loa.
Passengers: 491-third plus 743 temporary steerage berths.
Crew: 288.
Engines: quadruple expansion steam reciprocating, 9,500ihp (exhaust steam turbines added 1929, 12,000ihp); twin screw, 15kt.
Fate: broken up at Barrow-in-Furness, May 1936.

Barrabool (1923-36)
Harland & Wolff, Belfast, launched 3 November 1921.
13,148grt; 537ft loa.
Passengers: 491-third plus 743 temporary steerage berths.
Crew: 288.
Engines: quadruple expansion steam reciprocating, 9,500ihp (exhaust steam turbines added 1929, 12,000ihp); twin screw, 15kt.
Fate: broken up at Bo'ness, Firth of Forth, July 1936.

Moldavia (1922-38)
Cammell Laird, Birkenhead, launched 1 October 1921.
16,436grt; 573ft loa.
Passengers: (as built) 222-first, 175-second, (from 1931) 830-tourist.
Crew: 350.
Engines: geared steam turbines, 13,250shp; twin screw, 16kt.
Fate: broken up, April 1938.

Mongolia (1923-65)
Armstrong Whitworth, Walker-on-Tyne, launched 24 August 1922.
16,385grt; 568ft loa.
Passengers: (as built) 231-first, 180-second, (from 1931) 800-tourist.
Crew: 353.
Engines: geared steam turbines, 13,250shp; twin screw, 16kt.
Fate: chartered to New Zealand SS Co as Rimutaka (May 1938); sold for further trading, Europa (1950), Nassau (1951), Acapulco (1961); broken up in Japan, December 1965.

Mooltan (1923-54)
Harland & Wolff, Belfast, launched 15 February 1923.
20,952grt; 625ft loa.
Passengers: (as built) 327-first, 329-second, (from 1948) 1,030-tourist.
Crew: 422.
Engines: quadruple expansion steam reciprocating, 16,000ihp (exhaust turbo-electric machinery added 1929); twin screw, 17kt.
Fate: broken up at Faslane, January 1954.

Maloja (1924-54)
Harland & Wolff, Belfast, launched 19 April 1923.
20,914grt; 625ft loa.
Passengers: (as built) 327-first, 329-second, (from 1948) 1,030-tourist.
Crew: 422.
Engines: quadruple expansion steam reciprocating, 16,000ihp (exhaust steam turbines added 1929); twin screw, 17kt.
Fate: broken up at Inverkeithing, April 1954

Razmak (1925-60)
Harland & Wolff, Greenock, launched 16 October 1924.
10,852grt; 519ft loa.
Passengers: 142-first, 142-second.
Crew: 252.
Engines: quadruple expansion steam reciprocating with exhaust steam turbines, 12,000ihp; twin screw, 18kt.
Fate: transferred to Union SS Co of New Zealand as Monowai (November 1930); broken up, September 1960.

Cathay (1925-42)
Barclay Curle, Glasgow, launched 31 October 1924.

15,272grt; 545ft loa.
Passengers: 203-first, 103-second.
Crew: 278.
Engines: quadruple expansion steam
    reciprocating, 13,000ihp; twin screw, 16kt.
Fate: bombed and sunk off Bougie, Algeria,
    11 November 1942.

Comorin (1925-41)
Barclay Curle, Glasgow, launched 31 October
    1924.
15,279grt; 545ft loa.
Passengers: 203-first, 103-second.
Crew: 278.
Engines: quadruple expansion steam
    reciprocating, 13,000ihp (exhaust steam
    turbines added 1930); twin screw, 16kt.
Fate: destroyed by fire and sunk mid-Atlantic,
    6 April 1941.

Chitral (1925-53)
Alexander Stephen, Glasgow, launched 27
    January 1925.
15,396grt; 548ft loa.
Passengers: (as built) 199-first, 135-second,
    (from 1947) one-class.
Crew: 278.
Engines: quadruple expansion steam
    reciprocating, 13,000ihp (exhaust steam
    turbines added 1930); twin screw, 16kt.
Fate: broken up at Dalmuir, April 1953.

Ranpura (1925-61)
Hawthorn Leslie, Newcastle, launched
    13 September 1924.
16,688grt; 570ft loa.
Passengers: 310-first, 280-second.
Crew: 380.
Engines: quadruple expansion steam
    reciprocating, 15,000ihp (exhaust steam
    turbines added 1930); twin screw, 17kt.
Fate: purchased by the Admiralty as fleet repair
    ship HMS Ranpura, 1942; broken up at La
    Spezia, 1961.

Ranchi (1925-53)
Hawthorn Leslie, Newcastle, launched
    24 January 1925.
16,738grt; 570ft loa.
Passengers: (as built) 308-first, 282-second,
    (from 1948) one-class.
Crew: 380.
Engines: quadruple expansion steam
    reciprocating, 15,000ihp (exhaust steam
    turbines added 1931); twin screw, 17kt.
Fate: broken up at Newport, South Wales,
    January 1953.

Rawalpindi (1925-39)
Harland & Wolff, Greenock, launched 26 March
    1925.
16,697grt; 568ft loa.
Passengers: 310-first, 290-second.
Crew: 380.
Engines: quadruple expansion steam
    reciprocating, 15,000ihp (exhaust steam
    turbines added 1931); twin screw, 16kt.
Fate: shelled and sunk by German battlecruisers
    Gneisenau and Scharnhorst off Iceland,
    23 November 1939

Rajputana (1925-41)
Harland & Wolff, Greenock, launched 6 August
    1925.
16,644grt; 568ft loa.
Passengers: 307-first, 288-second.
Crew: 380.
Engines: quadruple expansion steam
    reciprocating, 15,000ihp (exhaust steam
    turbines added 1930); twin screw, 16kt.
Fate: torpedoed and sunk by submarine U108,
    west of Ireland, 13 April 1941.

Viceroy of India ex-Taj Mahal (1929-42)
Alexander Stephen, Glasgow, launched
    15 September 1928;
19,648grt; 612ft loa.
Passengers: 415-first, 258-second.
Crew: 420.
Engines: turbo-electric, 17,000shp; twin screw,
    19kt.
Fate: torpedoed and sunk by submarine U407,
    off Oran, Algeria, 11 November 1942.

Strathnaver (1931-62)
Vickers Armstrong, Barrow-in-Furness, launched
    5 February 1931.
22,547grt; 664ft loa.
Passengers: (as built) 500-first, 670-tourist;
    (from 1948) 573-first, 496-tourist; (from
    1954) 1,252-tourist.
Crew: 487.
Engines: turbo-electric, 28,000shp; twin screw,
    21kt.
Fate: broken up at Hong Kong, April 1962

Strathaird (1932-61)
Vickers Armstrong, Barrow-in-Furness, launched
    18 July 1931.
22,270grt; 664ft loa.
Passengers: (as built) 498-first, 668-tourist;
    (from 1946) 573-first, 496-tourist; (from
    1954) 1,242-tourist.
Crew: 490.
Engines: turbo-electric, 28,000shp; twin screw,
    21kt.
Fate: broken up at Hong Kong, July 1961.

Carthage ex-Canton (1931-61)
Alexander Stephen, Glasgow, launched
    18 August 1931.
14,304grt; 540ft loa.
Passengers: (as built) 175-first, 196-second;
    (from 1948) 181-first, 213-tourist.
Engines: geared steam turbines, 14,000shp; twin
    screw, 18kt.
Fate: broken up at Osaka, Japan as Carthage
    Maru, May 1961.

Corfu ex-Cheefoo (1931-61)
Alexander Stephen, Glasgow, launched 20 May
    1931.
14,293grt; 540ft loa.
Passengers: (as built) 178-first, 200-second;
    (from 1948) 181-first, 213-tourist.
Engines: geared steam turbines, 14,000shp; twin
    screw, 18kt.
Fate: broken up at Osaka, Japan as Corfu Maru,
    1961.

Strathmore (1935-69)
Vickers Armstrong, Barrow-in-Furness, launched
    4 April 1935.
23,428grt; 665ft loa.
Passengers: (as built) 445-first, 665-tourist;
    (from 1949) 497-first, 487-tourist; (from
    1961) 1,200-tourist.
Crew: 515.
Engines: geared steam turbines, 28,000shp; twin
    screw, 20kt.
Fate: sold for further trading, Marianna Latsi
    (1963), Henrietta Latsi (1966); broken up at
    La Spezia, May 1969.

Stratheden (1937-69)
Vickers Armstrong, Barrow-in-Furness, launched
    10 June 1937.
23,732grt; 664ft loa.
Passengers: (as built) 448-first, 563-tourist;
    (from 1947) 527-first, 453-tourist, (from
    1961) 1,200-tourist.
Crew: 563.
Engines: geared steam turbines, 28,000shp; twin
    screw, 20kt.
Fate: sold for further trading, Henrietta Latsi
    (1964), Marianna Latsi (1966); broken up at
    La Spezia, May 1969.

Strathallan (1938-42)
Vickers Armstrong, Barrow-in-Furness, launched
    23 September 1937.
23,722grt; 668ft loa.
Passengers: 448-first, 563-tourist.
Crew: 563.
Engines: geared steam turbines, 28,000shp; twin
    screw, 20kt.

Fate: torpedoed and sunk by submarine *U562*, off Oran, Algeria, 21 December 1942.

Ettrick (1939-42)
Barclay Curle, Glasgow, launched 25 August 1938.
11,279grt; 517ft loa.
Passengers: 104-first, 90-second, 1,150 troops.
Engines: 2-stroke, single-acting diesels; twin screw, 15kt.
Fate: torpedoed and sunk by submarine *U155*, 120 miles from Gibraltar, 15 November 1942

Canton (1938-62)
Alexander Stephen, Glasgow, launched 14 April 1938.
15,784grt; 563ft loa.
Passengers: (as built) 260-first, 220-second; (from 1947) 298-first, 244-tourist.
Crew: 370.
Engines: geared steam turbines, 18,500shp; twin screw, 18kt.
Fate: broken up at Hong Kong, October 1962.

Empire Fowey ex-Empire Jewel, ex-Potsdam (1935-76)
Blohm & Voss, Hamburg, launched 16 January 1935.
19,121grt; 634ft loa.
Passengers: (for P&O) 153-first, 94-second, 92-third, 1,297 troops.
Engines: geared steam turbines, 18,000shp (NB turbo-electric, 32,500shp as built); twin screw, 18kt.
Fate: sold for further trading, *Safina-E-Hujjaj* (1960); broken up at Gadani Beach, October 1976.

Himalaya (1949-74)
Vickers Armstrong, Barrow-in-Furness, launched 5 October 1948.
28,047grt; 709ft loa.
Passengers: (as built) 758-first, 401-tourist; (from 1963) 1,416-tourist.
Crew: 631.
Engines: geared steam turbines, 42,500shp; twin screw, 22kt.
Fate: broken up at Kaohsiung, Taiwan, November 1974.

Chusan (1950-73)
Vickers Armstrong, Barrow-in-Furness, launched 28 June 1949.
24,318grt; 673ft loa.
Passengers: (as built) 475-first, 551-tourist; (from 1960) 464-first, 541-tourist.
Crew: 572.

Engines: geared steam turbines, 42,500shp; twin screw, 22kt.
Fate: broken up at Kaohsiung, Taiwan, June 1973.

Arcadia (1954-79)
John Brown, Clydebank, launched 14 May 1953.
29,871grt; 721ft loa.
Passengers: 675-first, 735-tourist.
Crew: 710.
Engines: geared steam turbines, 42,500shp; twin screw, 22kt.
Fate: broken up at Kaohsiung, Taiwan, February 1979.

Iberia (1954-72)
Harland & Wolff, Belfast, launched 21 January 1954.
29,779grt; 718ft loa.
Passengers: 673-first, 733-tourist.
Crew: 711.
Engines: geared steam turbines, 42,500shp; twin screw, 22kt.
Fate: broken up at Kaohsiung, Taiwan, September 1972.

Chitral ex-Jadotville (1956-75)
Chantiers et Ateliers de Saint Nazaire, launched 30 November 1955.
13,821grt; 557ft loa.
Passengers: 231 one-class.
Crew: 196.
Engines: geared steam turbines, 12,500shp; single screw, 16.5kt.
Fate: transferred to Eastern & Australian SS Co in 1970; broken up in Taiwan, 1975.

Cathay ex-Baudouinville (1957-date)
Cockerill Ougree, Hoboken, launched 10 January 1957.
13,922grt; 559ft loa.
Passengers: 231 one-class.
Crew: 196.
Engines: geared steam turbines, 12,500shp; single screw, 16.5kt.
Fate: transferred to Eastern & Australian SS Co in 1970; sold for further trading, *Kengshin* (1976), *Shanghai* (1978); still in service.

Canberra (1961-97)
Harland & Wolff, Belfast, launched 16 March 1960.
45,733grt; 820ft loa.
Passengers: 548 first-class, 1,650 tourist-class.
Crew: 900.
Engines: turbo-electric, 88,000shp; twin screw, 27kt.
Fate: broken up at Gadani Beach, Pakistan, October 1997.

Orion (1935-63)
Vickers Armstrong, Barrow, launched 7 December 1934.
23,696grt; 665ft loa.
Passengers: 342 cabin-class, 722 tourist-class.
Crew: 466.
Engines: geared steam turbines, 24,000shp; twin screw, 20kt.
Fate: broken up in Belgium, November 1963 after brief spell as an hotel ship at Hamburg.

Orcades (1948-73)
Vickers Armstrong, Barrow, launched 14 October 1947.
28,399grt; 709ft loa.
Passengers: (from 1959) 631 first-class, 734 tourist-class; (from 1964) 1,635 tourist-class.
Engines: geared steam turbines, 42,500shp; twin screw, 22kt.
Fate: broken up at Kaohsiung, Taiwan, February 1973.

Oronsay (1951-75)
Vickers Armstrong, Barrow, launched 30 June 1950.
28,136grt; 708ft loa.
Passengers: 668 first-class, 833 tourist-class.
Crew: 622.
Engines: geared steam turbines, 42,500shp; twin screw, 22kt.
Fate: broken up at Kaohsiung, Taiwan, October 1975.

Orsova (1954-74)
Vickers Armstrong, Barrow, launched 14 May 1953.
29,091grt; 723ft loa.
Passengers: 681 first-class, 813 tourist-class.
Crew: 620.
Engines: geared steam turbines, 42,500shp; twin screw, 22kt.
Fate: broken up at Kaohsiung, Taiwan, February 1974.

Oriana (1960-86)
Vickers Armstrong, Barrow, launched 3 November 1959.
41,920grt; 804ft loa.
Passengers: 638 first-class, 1,496 tourist-class.
Crew: 903.
Engines: geared steam turbines, 80,000shp; twin screw, 27kt.
Fate: sold for use as a stationary tourist centre at Beppu, Kyushu, Japan, 1986

Maritime books from Ian ✈ Allan PRINTING

Glory Days: P&O
By David L. Williams ISBN: 0711026084 184mm x 240mm H/B **£14.99**

Glory Days: Cunard
By David L. Williams ISBN: 0711026076 184mm x 240mm H/B **£14.99**

Titanic — The Ship That Never Sank?
By Robin Gardiner ISBN: 0711026335 229mm x 1520mm H/B **£16.99**

Ocean Ships (1998 edition)
By David Hornsby ISBN: 0711025673 235mm x 172mm H/B **£18.99**

Sea Battles in Close-Up: World War 2 — Volume 1
By Martin Stephens ISBN: 0711015961 235mm x 172mm H/B **£19.99**

Sea Battles in Close-Up: World War 2 — Volume 2
By Eric Grove ISBN: 071102118X 235mm x 172mm H/B **£19.99**

Sea Battles in Close-Up: The Age of Nelson
By David Lyon ISBN: 0711022836 235mm x 172mm H/B **£19.99**

U-Boats Under The Swastika
By Jak P. Mallmann-Showell ISBN: 0711016828 235mm x 172mm H/B **£16.99**

US Carriers at War
By Peter Kilduff ISBN: 0711010773 292mm x 216mm H/B **£19.99**